DEER MAN

DEER MAN

Seven Years of Living in the Wild

GEOFFROY DELORME

Little, Brown

LITTLE, BROWN

First published in Great Britain in 2022 by Little, Brown

1 3 5 7 9 10 8 6 4 2

A CIP catalogue record for this book
is available from the British Library.

Hardback ISBN 978-1-4087-1480-5

Typeset in Goudy by M Rules
Printed and bound in Great Britain by Clays Ltd, Elcograf S.p.A.

Papers used by Little, Brown are from well-managed forests
and other responsible sources.

Little, Brown
An imprint of
Little, Brown Book Group
Carmelite House
50 Victoria Embankment
London EC4Y 0DZ

An Hachette UK Company
www.hachette.co.uk

www.littlebrown.co.uk

To Chévi, my best friend.

You taught me to live, to feel, to love,
to believe that everything was possible
and to become myself.

Dawn

Nature is all that we see,
All that we want, all that we love.
All that we know, all that we believe,
All that we feel within ourselves.
It is beautiful for those who see it,
Good to those who love it,
Just when we believe in it
And respect it within ourselves
Look at the sky, it sees you,
Kiss the earth, it loves you.
The truth is what we believe
In nature it's yourself.

GEORGE SAND

DEER MAN

Love of nature started as a
child.. loving to go into the
nearby woods day & nite..
Learning thru books all he
could about nature. Knowing
that nature called like a magnet.
   1st encounter in the woods
with a male deer ⇒ lesson—
animals meant me no harm
   After this encounter he daily
went into the woods to be with the
animals & nature. He knew
life in the woods awaited him.
   At 16 spent more time in the
woods. His life was filled with joy
& wonder & serenity.
   Finally decided to go into the
forest to live. Ate different plants
& nuts (rich in nutrition)

PROLOGUE

Is it a man or a woman? My eyes long ago lost the ability to spot that kind of detail from more than thirty metres away. Is that an animal running along beside them? Oh no, please, not a dog! I've got to stop them before they scare my friends away.

Like them, I've become very territorial. Anyone who enters my territory is seen as a threat. I feel as if my intimacy is being violated. My area of the forest has a radius of five kilometres. As soon as I see somebody I follow them, I spy on them, I collect information. If they come back too often, I'll do everything I can to scare them off.

I emerge from the undergrowth, determined to keep the walker from advancing any further. A strong smell of very sweet violets assaults my nostrils. My walker must be a woman. As I climb back up the little forest path, I realise that it's been months since I last addressed a word to a human being. I've been living in the forest for seven years, communicating only with animals. For the first few years I went back and forth between human society and the wilderness, but over time I ended up turning my back once and for all on what they call 'civilisation' to join my real family: roe deer.

As I advance along the little forest path, feelings rise up in me that I thought I had completely eliminated from my life. What must I look like? My hair hasn't seen a comb for years, and it's been cut 'blind', with a small pair of sewing scissors. Luckily my face is beardless. So there's that. My clothes? My trousers, completely covered in soil, could stand up all on their own like a sculpture. Well, at least it's dry today. At the beginning of my adventure I would sometimes check my reflection in a pocket mirror that I kept in a little round box. But over time, with the cold, the damp, the mirror tarnished and, to tell the truth, I no longer know what I look like.

It's a woman. I have to be polite so as not to frighten her. *But stay on your guard, you never know.* What word should I start with? 'Hello'; 'hello' is good. No, maybe 'good evening'. It's already the end of the day.

'Good evening . . .'

'Good evening, *monsieur.*'

1

As A child

I was very small when I discovered, in my first class in primary school, the foundations of my future human life – I was learning to read, to write, to count and how to behave in society – I could easily find myself looking out of the window, contemplating the nobility of life in the wild. I observed sparrows, robins, blue tits, any animal that passed through my field of vision, and I thought about how lucky those little creatures were to enjoy such freedom. I was shut away in this room with other children who seemed to like it there, while from my lofty six-year-old perspective I already aspired to that freedom. Obviously I was aware of how rough life out there must be, but when I observed that existence, simple and serene despite all its dangers, I felt a tiny germ of mutiny stirring within me, resisting a vision of human life in which I already felt they were attempting to confine me. Every day I spent by that window at the back of the class took me a little further away from what are known as 'societal' values, while the wild world exerted an attraction on me like a magnet on a compass needle.

Only a few months after the end of the holidays, an apparently banal event would give shape to that germ of rebellion. One fine morning I learned as I got to class that a trip to the swimming pool was planned. Somewhat timid by nature, I was already apprehensive. When we got to the pool itself I froze with horror. It was the first time I'd seen so much water, and, never having swum in my life, I was filled with an instinctive fear. All the other children seemed perfectly at ease, while I was gritting my teeth. The instructor, a red-haired woman with a long, severe face, asked me to get into the water. I refused. Her face tightened, her voice hardened, and she ordered me to jump in. I again refused. Then she walked heavily towards me like a military officer, took me by the hand and hurled me violently into the pool. I swallow great gulps of water, of course, and not knowing how to swim I started to go under. Gesticulating frantically, I saw my tormentor swimming in my direction. I panicked, certain that she was going to kill me. My survival instinct led me to do the impossible: I doggy-paddled to the middle of the pool and dived below the divider separating me from the larger pool with a view to reaching the other side. Having got to the edge, I climbed the ladder and ran as fast as I could to seek refuge in the changing rooms. I put my trousers and my t-shirt back on. Once she was back out of the water, the instructor looked for me everywhere. The sound of her footsteps on the damp tiles suggested that she was coming back up the little corridor that ran between the booths arranged on each side. I'd locked myself in the third one on the left. She flung open the second door, which closed again just as violently, an almighty racket that made me think she was smashing in each door in turn. Seized by panic, I started crawling from one booth to another, slipping through the spaces between wall and floor. Having reached the end of the row, I took advantage of the few seconds during which she examined one of the compartments to cross to the other side and slip discreetly out of the exit. Once outside I went charging down the street, running straight ahead, my eyes blurry with tears and chlorine, until a familiar-looking man stopped and asked me to go with him, taking me by the hand. It was the bus driver. He had seen me coming out by myself and had the presence of mind to follow me. Between hiccupping sobs I told him what had happened, and why I never wanted to go back to the pool. His voice and his words reassured me a little. Once my little drama was over and the teacher had been told how my flight had ended, I found myself at the back of the bus, alone, being stared by both teachers and classmates, like a dangerous wild animal that needed to be treated with care. After that incident, the decision was made to take me out of school. I would pursue my education at home thanks to the National Centre for Distance Education (CNED).

So I found myself alone in my room, isolated from the outside world, with no friends and no teachers. Luckily a big library was open to me, full of literary treasures (Nicolas Vanier, Jacques Cousteau, Dian Fossey, Jane Goodall, etc.), telling stories of nature and life in the wild. I also devoured

home schooling after swiming incident

library nature book

all the popular science books I could get my hands on (*Nature Day After Day, Survival of the Fittest, Woodland Friends*). A mine of precious information that I tried to apply on my own personal scale, in my garden. An apple tree, a plum tree, a cherry tree, barberry hedges, cotoneasters, pyracanthas, a few rose bushes – there were all kinds of things around the family home to stop me getting bored. Tending to all that plant life quickly became my main source of escape.

One morning I discovered that blackbirds had made their nest in the hedge opposite my bedroom. In my childish brain, that discovery produced an overriding command: I had to look after them. I started doing my rounds along the hedge like a car-park attendant, shooing away the cats attracted by the scent of easy prey. At all times of the day and night, as soon as I was sure no adults were watching me, I would open my window and slip outside, as discreet as a cat, in search of news of my little feathered family. Seeing me so often, they seemed to have got used to me. I gave them food, bread-crumbs, earthworms or insects that I put on a little plate. The parent birds came and picked at them and brought them to the fledgelings. With each passing day I gained their trust a little more. Now I could actually go inside the hedge to watch the babies squawking, my face only six inches from theirs. When the moment finally came for them to leave the nest, it was the father who left first. The little ones jumped out behind him and fell to the ground. The mother bird brought up the rear. They all hopped around the hedge. Sometimes they would approach me. I felt as if they were trying to introduce themselves. My nine-year-old's heart hammered. It was my first contact with the wild world and to immortalise it I took a photograph of the fledgelings and sent it to my examiner at CNED, Mme Krieger.

Each time I went for a walk I would extend my exploration of the surrounding area a little further. Behind the hedge there was a fence beneath which a hole had been dug, presumably by foxes. I slipped through it without any difficulty, to discover the neighbouring field and the promises of adventure that went with it. The first few times, at night, by the moon's faint light, the thirst for freedom was always tinged with fear, the burning instinct of the little adventurer always reined in by the prudence of the good little boy. But the irresistible draw of nature soon tipped the balance towards life in the wild. And on that new playing field all my senses were awakened. Concentrating on my walk, I registered the topography and the nature of the ground. Every evening, touch replaced vision, and my body learned the terrain until I could map its contours with my eyes closed. It was exactly the same memorising process that the body uses when we get up in the dark and know exactly where the light switch is, except that in this case I was applying it in the middle of the countryside. The smells changed, too. Nettles, for example, smelled much stronger at night. Even the earth didn't give off the same perfume. And when I sniffed the damp exhalations of the marsh of the Petit-Saint-Ouen, I knew that my jaunt would soon be over. If I pressed on a little further, I would reach the forest ranger's house. And beyond that lay the forest, the unknown.

He learned terrain until he had a map in his minds eye.

Pine forest. I used to come here when a storm was raging. The pines acted as an effective windbreak, often producing a microclimate. It could add one or two degrees. The pine cones and the needles that had fallen on the ground made it easy for me to light fires.

The nightjars circled around my head, their flight producing a curious humming, harsh and monotonous. I wasn't afraid. I felt great.

Deep within me there was an instinct for freedom that made me escape as soon as the opportunity presented itself. And one single rule seemed worthy of respect: that of nature. I never broke a branch; I wouldn't even touch dead trees. I made up increasingly sophisticated rituals, bordering the absurd, because I had an inexplicable sense that the events I was witnessing were more striking and more frequent when I passed the trees on their right. So I constructed my imaginary world, my spirituality, my relationship with nature, all well-documented, well-thought-out and filled with a childish mysticism.

For some time, a fox had regularly been sleeping under a leafy tree in our garden. One winter evening I decided to follow it across the fields. As it reached the forest ranger's house, I saw it carrying on along its route at a gentle trot. It was time to dive into the unknown. About a hundred yards further off, on the edge of the forest, a cub revealed to me the entrance to its den. I had never ventured so far from my bedroom. The wind, still blowing in the same direction, carried all the scents in from the field. Suddenly the twilight thickened. The sound changed, too. There were countless new sounds, because life was there, in the depths of the wood. I stepped inside a little way, ten metres, then ten more, just long enough to feel that little shiver of adrenaline that something mysterious gives you, before turning on my heels. There was, in fact, nothing to fear. The animals knew very well that the fields were the thing you should be wary of. The forest was fascinating, enchanting. I ventured a little further in each evening, always cautiously, as if to avoid offending it. Then one night I found myself face to face with a red deer. I'd often heard them braying at the end of the summer, but I'd never dared approach them. Their hoarse bellowing at night was too intimidating for a little ten-year-old boy. And that unexpected encounter petrified me. That heavy body less than ten metres away from me, the ground shaking with each step he took: I was overwhelmed by the power emanating from the creature. My heartbeat must have been audible a long way off. Suddenly it turned towards me and started braying with that hoarse voice. Around him, the does started replying in tones that were slightly less deep but just as loud. Each bray made my ribcage vibrate, like the low frequencies of a stereo channel. In the end the stag turned away. I did the same, to show him that I hadn't just come to see him. And we left each other like that, two creatures that had met by chance while wandering at night. Slipping silently under my covers a few moments later, I realised that the stag had given me the finest lesson of my short life: animals meant me no harm. I already wanted to go back, but I had to be patient. The wild world doesn't open itself up to just anybody.

From then on, as soon as the house was asleep, I opened my bedroom window, slipped behind the blackbird hedge and crossed the nightjar field to find the gloom of the big trees and the bustle of the animals. The foxes that were the first to lead me there revealed their burrowing neighbours, badgers. Above my head I discovered other life. If there is one bone-chilling creature in the forest it's definitely the owl. A silent predator that isn't afraid of anything or anybody. Amid the constant murmur of the forest you can't hear it fly, and if you rouse its curiosity it will have no hesitation in coming right over to you. The first time I crossed paths with an owl I was still recovering from the Dante-esque scenes in the film *Jurassic Park*. Without my noticing, the creature had settled on a branch less than two metres from me. All of a sudden, without warning, it made its 'hoo-hoo' cry. I started backwards, tripping over a log, landing with my feet in the air, my eyes wide and my backside in the mud. The night life of the forest is thrilling. Many animals, both small and big, get on with their daily tasks at night. But some of them never seem to rest. This is true of the squirrels that I see strolling around my garden during the day and running in all directions at night. When do they find the time to sleep? The question obsessed me until I worked out what I was failing to understand. Flicking through a picture book about the world of the forest, I realised that the hyperactive little rodents that I observed at night weren't squirrels at all, but young dormice. I was misled by their tufty little tails.

All those elements of my childhood were there as if to tell me that life in the wild awaited me somewhere, and that when I was able to shed the burden of human constraints the forest would be there to welcome me. I believed so firmly in that prophecy that I sometimes went to sleep with my fists clenched very tightly, praying for night to turn me into a fox so that in the early hours, when my bedroom window opened, I would be able to escape by trotting towards that woodland vastness that inspired my dreams. The reality was much less exciting. I lived almost entirely alone, without friends or classmates, without holidays or school trips, and apart from my nocturnal escapades I sat in my room studying by correspondence with teachers at the other end of France, or going on little cycle rides around the garden. On my rare permitted outings, to go shopping, for example, I would sometimes talk to the various shopkeepers who quizzed me about this home schooling business. I told them all that the situation suited me perfectly, because even if deep down I had a sense that something wasn't quite right, I had no way of comparing myself to other children.

The truth is that the life imposed upon me gradually turned into a form of moral torture. So much so that at the age of sixteen I took the decision to spend not only my nights but also my days in the forest. And my rebellion reached its peak on the day of the tests for the *Baccalauréat*, the school leaving exam. I decided to scupper the educational boat once and for all by throwing my registration letter into a maize field. Over those past few years I had discovered a passion for nature illustration, and wanted to start training as a draughtsman. Except that the school wanted me to study 'business practice and communication'. I didn't even know what the words meant. Finally, battle-weary, I agreed to sign up for a course of study for apprentice sales staff, which included by way of consolation a photography correspondence course. My passion for wild fauna remained intact, and I planned to do something with it. Over the course of my forest outings, I became aware that the wild animals recognised my scent, my various postures. They welcomed me into their habitat until I was basically part of the scenery. It took me a long time; I spent whole days and weeks in the forest, claiming that I was engaged in a long photography course. When I got home I was told that what I was doing wasn't a job, it wasn't something I could make a living from. But money wasn't my priority. My quest was for a certain moral stability. Living in the present moment like the forest animals gave me my true place in the order of things. Animals showed me that the more I thought, the more filled I was with a sense of danger. The problems of my past, or those bound up with the uncertainty of my future, along with my desire to keep hold of the mastery of the present without ever letting go, were slowly destroying me. Observing the nature around me and absorbing the wild world stirred my mind in a thousand ways and clarified my thoughts.

For several months I had not been aware of the time, the hours and days, spent in the forest. My life was more intense, and filled with joy, wonder and serenity. That didn't mean that I jettisoned all sense of reality, though. To avoid sinking into morbid destitution I did some sports photography for local newspapers, which allowed me to buy clothes and food. Obviously nobody believed in me and I had no moral support. My parents tried to tempt me by saying that the 'herd' would protect me, that I wouldn't survive for long on my own. But the more they tried to hold me back, the more frayed the bonds became. And then one day they broke. The decision was made: I was going into the forest. A Jean de La Fontaine fable gives quite a precise description of what I felt at that moment. It's called 'The Wolf and the Dog', and this is the story it tells:

> *A wolf was all skin and bone*
> *So well did the dogs keep watch.*
> *The wolf met a mastiff as strong as it was handsome,*
> *Fat and shiny, which had lost its way.*
> *The wolf would happily have torn it to bits;*
> *But battle was called for*
> *And the mastiff was big enough*
> *To defend itself most boldly.*
> *So the wolf approached it humbly,*
> *Addressed the dog and complimented it*
> *Upon its fatness, which it admired.*
> *It's up to you, my fine fellow,*
> *To be as fat as me, the dog replied.*
> *Leave the woods and you will do well;*
> *Your peers are miserable there.*
> *Thin and mangy, poor wretches they are,*
> *Destined to die of hunger.*
> *For they have no elegant water jugs*
> *And always face death by the sword.*
> *Follow me: a better fate awaits you.*
> *The wolf replied: what do I need to do?*

Hardly anything, said the dog; chase people carrying
    sticks, and beggars;
Flatter the ones with houses, please their masters:
As the result of which your wages
Will be rich in every way:
Chicken bones, pigeon bones,
Not to mention occasional strokes.
The wolf was already imagining a happiness
That made it weep with tenderness.
As they walked on it saw the dog's collar:
What's that, it said. – Nothing. – What? Nothing? –
    Hardly anything.
– But what? – The collar by which I am attached
From what you see may be the cause.
– Attached? the wolf said. So you can't run
Where you wish? – Not always; but what does
    that matter?
– It matters in that I wish nothing
Of all your meals,
At that price I would not wish a treasure.
Having said which our wolf ran away, and runs still.

And the moral of this story: it is better to be poor and free
than rich and fettered

2

My expedition into the woodland realm began in April and I decided, where possible, to eat only locally grown fare, following an omnivorous but vegetarian-inclined diet. I could not imagine living in a natural habitat and eating the wild animals that lived there. My human values had not abandoned me, and I was aware of the importance of respecting others, even though I admit that nature is overflowing with predators that have no choice but to kill in order to feed themselves and survive. To find food in the forest, I needed above all to create for myself a territory that provided a concentration of food and shelter. So initially my ambition was to reproduce the way in which squirrels looked after themselves. With the money I had saved from my photographic work, I bought tins of food, drinking water and the equipment that I thought I would need to survive in what we must, if we are honest, call a rather hostile environment. I hid everything at the foot of a tree, amid a lacework of roots that I thought I alone knew about, under a pile of branches and dead leaves. Unfortunately, a few days later, wild boar discovered my hoard and revelled in it. All the tins were disembowelled by their razor-sharp trotters. My hoard was crushed, shattered, dissipated. Nothing survived the powerful trampling of the herd, which left behind it just a heap of debris, as if to say: 'And where do you think you are?' I was obviously shocked for a few minutes, and then I had to put things into perspective. Nature has funny ways of putting us in our place when necessary. From now on, to protect my scant possessions from the greedy and the curious, I would bury my little packages in old poachers' holes. Those cavities, about forty-five centimetres wide and two metres deep, were used in the past to trap foxes and badgers. I just had to remove the murderous snares at the bottom and cover them over with good solid wood to prevent walkers from falling in.

This anecdote also brought it home to me that going to the shops and bringing my shopping back into the depths of the forest in my fifty-litre rucksack was, frankly, exhausting. And exhaustion, when you are living outdoors, is something that should not be ignored. In fact, in order to survive, my most efficient strategy was to eat as far as possible what I already had at my disposal. Bramble, silver birch, hornbeam and bay leaves, 'dry' fruits such as chestnuts, beechnuts, seeds or hazelnuts, and also plantains, dandelions, sorrel and a huge number of other plants that taste more or less good but are extremely rich in nutrition. From now on, I would only eat food from the outside world if everything else was in short supply. It

Pine-cone battles. Squirrels are mischievous and territorial. They had no hesitation in throwing pine cones at me, and anything else within reach, to move me on when I was sleeping at the foot of their tree

even became something to celebrate when I brought it into
the forest; even a simple tin of ravioli.

There was one other source of gastronomic delight: the
food that hunters left at the foot of trees to fatten up the boar.
So I got the pumpkins, courgettes, tomatoes and other fruit
and vegetables, bread, too, unsalted but bread nonetheless.
It was by following the animals – boar, foxes, badgers – that
I discovered this form of pilfering. They were the ones with
experience, so they were also the ones that showed me the
way, and with every passing day I came a little closer to them,
I became a little wilder. Without being aware of it, I was per-
forming a study in animal behaviour (or ethology, to give it
its scientific name) in order to become, very gradually, a guest
of the forest. The boar, the red deer and the foxes that I came
across increasingly accepted me on their territory, while at
the same time keeping their distance. After a few months I
felt as if I had melted into the most marvellous scenery imag-
inable, the world of the forest. It was then that I made the
acquaintance of an enigmatic and fascinating creature, the
one that would quite simply open my eyes to life in the wild:
the roe deer.

One fine morning when I was plucking a few leaves to chew
on by the edge of a path, a roe deer, the one that I would
come to call by the French name Daguet (which translates as
'roebuck' in English), crossed my path and came to a stand-
still a few steps away from me. Very slowly, I crouched down.
I was fascinated by his big, shiny black eyes. He straightened
his head and pointed his ears in my direction. The hairs on

his scut bristled. We stared at one another for a few minutes, which seemed to me to last for hours. He looked sideways at me as if inviting me to join him in discovering the forest. He turned away slowly and elegantly and plunged into the under-growth. I had just been touched by something stronger than myself. I had felt the call of the forest. My knees trembled and my breathing became shallow. It was time for me to leave the world of human beings to live among the roe deer and learn to understand them.

3

'm eating from a bramble that provides a good supply of small leaves, slightly withered but very nourishing nonetheless. I've been savouring this salad for three-quarters of an hour when I spot Daguet's little face emerging from the bushes in front of me. Rather than running away as a normal roe deer would, Daguet chooses to stay and observe me. I tell myself that he must have been there for a while, because I didn't see him coming. After a few minutes I leave my bramble patch to go and have a rest, and pretend not to have noticed that he's there. He watches me leave and the day continues. In the evening, I take advantage of the cool of sunset to eat a few yarrow leaves in the clearing. Once again I happen upon Daguet, who is following me everywhere as if it is perfectly normal. His curiosity surprises me; he seems to have decided to find out more about this newcomer who has invited himself into his home. And from one day to the next our relationship grows along with our encounters in our shared territory.

DAGUET- BUCK

On one particular day I decide to try and walk behind him. With a cool north wind blowing through the still leafless canopy, Daguet is chewing the cud while lying at the foot of a tree. I approach him gently, picking the odd leaf here and there. I hide behind each tree in turn to avoid attracting attention. I repeat this several times and he still doesn't move. I've probably developed an unusual talent for approaching stealthily, unless, that is, he's pretending not to see me. Just to be sure, I come out to the left of the tree that I've been shelter-ing behind, to appear within his eyeline so that he can't miss me, then I approach him slowly, half crouching. He regards me calmly. It's almost unbelievable. The rascal has been mocking me from the very beginning, letting me advance from tree to tree like an idiot. When I'm about ten metres away Daguet gets to his feet and stretches. I stop. He considers me. And we stand like that for a good half-hour. It's an absolutely magical moment. I feed on his mere presence. I have a sense of total communion with him and all the other things that surround us. Daguet has made me a part of his environment, and I'm the first person to be granted such a privilege. My heart and soul are at peace. My brain is on hold. At that precise moment, the whole of my existence is governed by a single law: respect. After a few minutes, a first thought fills me: as long as we are not disturbed by other humans. It would be terrible if he associated me with them. The Native Americans used to say that when hunting roe deer you shouldn't think about them too much, in case they sense your thoughts and make their escape. That seems entirely reasonable to me. Thoughts

Daguet (buck) has allowed him to be part of his environment. 1st person to do so.

become mood and moods become scents. So I force myself to have positive thoughts, in the hope of making that silent dialogue with Daguet last for as long as possible.

After a while my legs go numb, and I'm not sure what to do, when at last he starts moving forward. I walk slowly behind him from a distance of about ten metres, still crouching. His ears point backwards, in my direction, alert for the slightest mistake. The dry leaves on the ground rustle under my weight and make him start a few times. He sets off at a trot and then stops again, turns around and waits for me. I find that thrilling. I'm having a unique moment with a wild animal that is trying to tame me. I stand upright and imagine the effort he must be making to resist his instinctive fear of man and not set off at a hundred kilometres an hour at the sight of this

Daguet. He's the very first roe deer to trust me. He was the one that opened the doors of the forest to me. This patch of forest was a large part of Daguet's territory. A ring road now runs through it.

five-foot-seven mass standing before him. Suddenly the bark of a roe deer can be heard in the distance. It must be Six-Points, another roe deer that I will come across regularly, who is also intrigued by my presence. Daguet reacts immediately to that bark and runs off towards it at such incredible speed that I find myself all on my own like a fool in the middle of the oak wood.

Sharing the lives of roe deer involves giving up a number of things. Generally speaking, you have to forget all about the human codes of life in society, such as saying 'goodbye' when you leave. You also have to give up on certain conventions like eating at a fixed time or sleeping at night. With Daguet I discovered the complexity of the night-time life of the forest, and tried to become as much a part of it as I could. But I was already becoming exhausted. I would have liked to have had the whole night to recover, but I woke up far too often and struggled to get back to sleep. The hooting owls, the screeching foxes, and particularly the boar made a terrible racket. They squeaked and screamed and grunted and ran in all directions. Last year's boarlets came and touched me playfully with the tips of their snouts before immediately running off again. But the worst enemy of sleep was the cold. Several times I suffered from hypothermia. It was the same every time. I would go to sleep, I would start dreaming, and all of a sudden I would wake up quite numb, feeling as if I was going to be sick. After a few weeks, the lack of sleep started to make me hallucinate. I would hear voices, see silhouettes, sometimes I even felt as if I was flying. I was quite honestly wiped out. My

COLD made sleep difficult

nerves were shot, my shoulders heavy and my head weighed at least a ton. Even worse, my eyesight was blurred. And I started asking myself serious questions as to how my adventure was going to end.

The problem was that I never rested. During the day I looked for my food and built little shelters to protect myself from the weather, which took an insane amount of time. The problem with a shelter is that it quickly attracts insects, so you have to rebuild it every day. One morning I decided to start all over again. If I wanted to survive I had to adopt a different strategy, a more efficient way of living. It was spring, and I still had two seasons to adapt before winter arrived, or else the expedition would stop right there. There must have been something I was missing, or something I was doing badly.

I found out the answers by observing Daguet. Roe deer rest for short cycles both during the day and at night; one or two hours depending on the weather. I decided to base the rhythm of my life on that of my fellow adventurer. When he got up it was to ingest an impressive amount of vegetation, then lie down, chew the cud (having only one stomach, I meditate instead), then sleep again. The rest of the time was reserved for playing, for survival, for reproduction or for territorial marking, depending on the season. Finally, it was by observing my roe deer friends that I learned that sleeping at night isn't compulsory, as long as you rest from time to time. To do that I would crouch down, preferably in a dry place, with my right hand on my left knee and my left hand on my right knee and my head between my arms. After a moment my mouth would fill with saliva and that would wake me up. As a result my body wouldn't have time to slip into hypothermia. And to compensate, like Daguet, I would sleep during the day for about two hours at a time. That would give me time to eat, and more importantly to build up some stores of wood all over the forest, because it was vital to be able to make a fire anywhere and at any time of night without having to look for wood. And that was how I worked out in the end that night in the forest is more important than day. The advantage of the night – animals understand this – is that you are no longer visible, and hence in less danger. You can relax your vigilance and move around more freely.

In the early morning, the sensation of seeing the sun rise over the meadow, making rainbows in the mist and the still frost-covered undergrowth, beside my delightful roe deer friend, was irreplaceable. A new man was being born within me, and that new man had chosen the path to freedom. Daguet welcomed me into his intimate world, and as I became a part of his way of life I discovered a roe deer brother who would soon become my real family.

Kept the modern world out as much as possible retaining only the necessities.

4

Never again will I question the turn that my life took the day I decided to live in the forest; I chose the only possible direction to take, impelled by the same force that led me towards the forest realm at a very young age. I didn't want to live out that adventure naked, like Robinson Crusoe in Michel Tournier's masterpiece *Friday, or The Other Island*, knocking stones against each other to make fire in defiance of all modern technology. Nonetheless, this curious expedition required a certain rigour, because my woodland friends very quickly became nervous. I had to keep their trust, and not yield too often to the temptation of returning to the human world to rest and recuperate for a few days. It was a constant will, in spite of the cold, the vagaries of the weather or hunger that held me in its grip. The lives of my little protégés passed before mine, and their willingness to continue the adventure with me would depend on my state of mind. So I kept the modern world out of the forest as much as possible, retaining only what was strictly necessary. First of all, a change of clothes to keep out the cold: two pairs of canvas trousers and a pair of jeans, alpaca wool underpants, linen or hemp t-shirts, virgin wool pullovers and two seaman's caps. I had abandoned cotton a long time ago, since it seemed impossible to dry. To keep them from rotting, I stored those clothes in sealed bags in a rucksack, buried in a strategic corner of the forest. For cooking, I used only a small aluminium frying pan and a pot for boiling water. I also had a survival knife for cutting, hollowing, carving, peeling and pruning. A solar charger for my camera as well as a cigarette lighter and my ID card, which I keep in a round metal case with a little mirror under the lid. A mirror is very useful, particularly when it comes to diagnosing an awkwardly placed insect bite on your foot or on your back.

I know I live in the age of the fleece jacket and everything made out of plastic, in a society that's addicted to overconsumption of everything at all times, devoted to a cult of waste and uselessness, a system that destroys the value of honour and of even the most decent human beings, based on an economy that is constantly on the brink of collapse. So obviously I find it reassuring to know what to eat in the forest, how to make a fire in winter, in rain or wind, how to build a shelter and everything I need to survive in the wild.

But be careful: complete autonomy is a goal that you only achieve over a very long period of time. It's not something you can improvise. The greatest difficulty lies in making it through the winter, a tricky season during which food is in

Gourmet. Unlike red deer, which browse large amounts of low-nutrition grass, roe deer are precise in their selection of food, in search of certain tannins that exist in plants and which are necessary for their health.

short supply. That means you have to learn to stock up. You begin by collecting plants in the spring. To dry them, after several failures (attacks by insects, rot and other undesirable fungi), I developed an almost infallible technique, using shopping nets hung from a branch during the day to take advantage of the sun, and Ziploc storage bags to avoid the damp at night. Nettle, mint, oregano, dead nettle, meadowsweet, yarrow, angelica ... Of course you also need to serve a full apprenticeship if you want to be certain that you can tell edible plants from poisonous ones, and have an idea of the energy value of each. Nobody normally picks angelica, for example. And for good reason, because it is almost indistinguishable from hemlock, the plant from which the ancient Athenians derived the official poison that they used in executions. Look what happened to Socrates. The same is true of wild garlic, a plant that is delicious and rich in minerals, but one that can be easily confused with meadow saffron. The problem with meadow saffron is that you can eat it and then sleep like a baby. The toxic effects only set in after a number of days, once the sly perennial has attacked your liver, which is bound in the end to explode. Care must be taken. The dock leaf, for example, is a very flavoursome plant, and pleasant to eat, but in large quantities it causes very bad indigestion. Apart from mineral salts, you need to think about proteins. The arrival of autumn marks the start of the harvest of chestnuts, hazelnuts, acorns and all the shelled fruits necessary for a balanced diet without animal protein. Storing these foodstuffs is easier. Like a little squirrel, I keep them in a rocky cave or in the hollow of a tree. Then there is the thorny issue of vitamins. The main source of these is in the fruits that we pick between spring and summer. Except that keeping fruit for any length of time is unimaginable without a sterilisation process that I don't have access to. The only solution consists in training my body to store vitamin C in order to get through the winter, just as animals do. The process may appear extreme. I have, however, tested it out over many long years. In short, as long as you have eked out your food store and not had too many accidents along the way, and as long as you have a reasonably resilient organism, you can expect to reach alimentary autonomy after a year or so.

In fact, my consumption of industrial foods shrunk progressively, as it was compensated for by foraging. I discovered the willowherb with its little flowers and edible root, which used to be called 'Heal-all'. You dig it out with a knife and eat it raw. There are also nettle roots, the little roots of the bramble, wild carrots. Let's be honest: at first it's frankly repellent. There is nothing simple about moving from a gastronomic world in which everything is saturated with sugar and salt to a harsh and bitter diet. All of those plants and roots are good for the health, but you can say goodbye to the idea of delighting your taste buds. The red dead nettle, for example, a plant whose concentration of proteins and trace elements is essential for survival in the forest, well, it tastes like a spoonful of compost. Even more surprising, comfrey, another protein-rich plant, tastes faintly of fish. Luckily, it's not all bad. After a few months, when you've lost the sweet taste of cornflakes, certain natural foods like clover flowers or silver birch sap reveal that they have very agreeable sweet notes.

To get through the winter, you have to battle not only hunger but also cold. And in that struggle I prefer to use natural materials that have stood the test of time. Sheep's wool, first of all, to protect myself against both low temperatures and storms. Only wool allows you to stay warm even when you're wet. Otherwise, I wear multiple layers of jumpers of different sizes and knits. The finest mesh pullover with a dense weave is a good imitation of the layer of fur that roe deer have. A second medium-mesh jumper over the first retains the warmth but allows the air to circulate and keep it from getting stale.

The third pullover is made of coarse wool. It keeps out damp and frost. When it rains, this layer gets soaked but without transmitting the moisture too quickly to other layers of pullovers. Then you just have to take that one off and dry it to rid it of the accumulated water before putting it back on again; since the body is warmer than the outside temperature, the water will evaporate naturally. I wear a parka only very rarely, because it allows contact between perspiration and the air, which produces an unpleasant sensation of penetrating cold and creates a higher risk of hypothermia. Under my trousers, my woollen underpants are very effective, like the cap and the gloves. My socks are made of alpaca wool too. Only my shoes, by Gore-Tex, are of a man-made fibre.

To live in harmony with roe deer, and to be able to walk behind them, I also cast off the swirling habit of thought, reflecting on my experiences. That's certainly the most difficult thing. But after a year I had come to see the human world as in a way ignorant. Alone in the forest with the roe deer I don't think about anything, I don't define in words that I see, breathe or hear. I am just happy to be there, with them, and to feel nature rather than to strip it bare. I speak very little, in order to leave room for intuition. I throw down the challenge to get to know Daguet by imitating him, observing him and trying to understand him. He seems just as curious to find out about me, if not more so. Then I leave room for feelings. Taking this opportunity to 'be' rather than to 'do' or to 'think'. When I manage to do that I very quickly fall under the spell of these cheeky and playful little creatures, which have

Forest. In the morning, the warmth from the gentle rays of sunlight allows you to dry after a night that may have been damp. Then the dew settles on the vegetation lining the path; it makes the leaves tender and succulent.

developed the skill and the habit of sometimes living at the expense of humans, often even venturing into our orchards or vegetable gardens. In order to immortalise those moments, and to make a family album later on, when I can I sometimes bring along a camera with rechargeable batteries. That means I can slip a few into my pocket and change them regularly. Unfortunately they don't last long in the cold, and my little charger isn't much use in a forest where the light is faint.

Adaptating to the natural environment is a long process that demands patience. Your metabolism changes. Your mind changes. Your reflexes change. Everything changes, but slowly. I have to accept being malleable, accept that my body will adapt, and that takes time. I mustn't try to control it because

living in the forest changes you.. metabolism /mind /reflexes /everything changes but slowly

that's not how things work. The forest is neither good nor bad, it just forces you to rethink yourself, constantly.

5

Roe deer are animals with routines, and rather than spend my time looking for them in the undergrowth and pointlessly using up my energy, such a precious gift when you live outdoors, I sit down by the side of a path along which, I know, a handsome deer I call Arrow will take advantage of the peace of the sunrise to nibble on some young shoots. The meadow is completely covered with frost, and the sun caresses my face, still frozen from that spring night. I feel the warmth of its rays warming my body, almost pierced through with the ambient humidity that is evaporating from my clothes. Territories take a long time to establish, and Arrow is on the alert. At regular intervals he lifts his head abruptly, turns around and sniffs the air, before returning to his main occupation of that moment: eating. Six-Points, having sensed a potential rival on his territory, crosses the avenue in front of me, trots in my direction, pauses, thinks for a second and then comes forward to pass me on my left. He goes on staring at me, neck stretched, eyes

suspicious as if to say: 'Hang on – what're you doing here?'
Then he continues on his way until he has reached his goal,
which is none other than poor Arrow. I'm not yet exactly
friends with Six-Points, but I've bumped into him on many
occasions, even before setting off to live in the forest full-time.
I know he's territorial, and that he's a difficult character. I
like to call him 'Growler' because he barks at everything that
moves. His companion, Star, a magnificent little doe with a
slender body and mischievous eyes, breaks my heart every time
I see her. She follows Six-Points at a few strides' distance and
seems much less enthusiastic than her companion about the
process of marking territory. I can tell by her slightly rounded
flanks that she is going to have some fawns this year, and I
think about the names I'm going to be able to give them.

Six-Points recognises Arrow, who is on the extreme edge
of his territory. Like human beings, roe deer have a rather
individualistic way of life and, during the phase of territorial
marking, they like to quarrel a little. Unfortunately for the
other bucks, territorial marking is an art at which Six-Points
is a past master. Once they are beyond the 'band of brothers'
stage, the youngest bucks often try and settle in a place that
offers them both food and protection by virtue of their being
the sole tenants. To accomplish this, the roebuck has to find
a tract of woodland beyond his rivals' territory and set about
defending it against intruders. Six-Point's and Arrow's territories are very close to one another, and overlap in places.
Plainly our two neighbours will have to sort things out, and
Six-Points is determined to get rid of this little upstart who's

*territorial – staking out an
area for food + protection*

been nibbling away at his personal flower beds. Six-Points regularly moistens his nostrils with his tongue and stands facing into the wind. Arrow, in spite of his vigilance, doesn't suspect anything and continues eating. Suddenly, with a bark that splits the dawn, Six-Points charges at Arrow. With an incredible leap, Arrow starts running and barks as well. His movements are chaotic, and in his panic he takes the wrong path, plunging further into the territory of Six-Points, who stops breathlessly for a moment, probably outraged that such arrogance is even possible. He sets off again, barking at the top of his voice, except that in spite of his lack of experience Arrow isn't called Arrow for nothing. He leaps over a fallen tree trunk, veers to the right, hurtles through a little thicket and disappears before the very eyes of Six-Points. Irritated and disappointed, he turns towards Star with a grunt of discontent, rubbing his head against all the surrounding vegetation to demonstrate even more clearly that this is Six-Points Land, and that no one can come in here without his permission,

does Star still seems entirely uninterested in this activity. But we shouldn't trust her little face, because I will learn later that does don't like other females on their territory either. Often the bucks create their domain in deference to the does. A roebuck will always ensure that his territory crosses the area of activity of several does so that during the rutting season in July/August he has – how can I put it – a choice. Similarly, while last year's fawns are still there, the doe will explain to them, sometimes clumsily, that it's time for them to lead their own lives from now on. Still, many mothers offer their daughters territories close to their own. Where possible, roe deer try to reconquer the same territory every year, but the logging business may have other ideas, felling entire areas of woodland and thus disturbing the cycle of territorial marking. That's what happened to Courage, Chévi's half-brother, whose story I'll discuss a bit later. In the spring, the roebuck leaves markers by scratching the ground with his front hoof, to impregnate the soil with the scent of his foot glands, what's known as 'scraping'. A few weeks later, when getting rid of the velvet covering his antlers, he vigorously rubs them against the straight, supple twigs of young shrubs, then polishes and anoints them with a scented substance secreted by the gland on his forehead so that the other deer are aware of his presence. This marking technique is known as the 'rub'. Then, when pacing out his territory, sometimes with surprising regularity, he rubs his muzzle against low vegetation to leave olfactory proof of his passage. The complete set of visual and olfactory markers allows the roe deer to demarcate his territory precisely.

The mist thickens and begins to obscure the sun; I abandon Six-Points and Star to go in search of Daguet.

The Forêt de Bord is a forest of 4,500 hectares located in the *département* of the Eure. Its horseshoe shape melds perfectly with the fourth bend in the Seine. If I travel from east to west, I pass through vegetation made up principally of pines and beech trees to reach a denser forest of oak and wild cherries. I chose to base myself in the east, on a big overhanging rock called la Crutte, which dominates the

Six-Points in the pines. Six-Points is the most territorial roe deer I've come across. He barks so often that I call him 'Growler'.

whole of the Seine valley all the way to the Deux Amants. This place, beloved of hikers, takes its name from a medieval poem that tells the tragic story of two lovers, Mathilde, daughter of the Baron de Cantelpou, and the young Raoul de Bonnemare. In order for him to win Mathilde's hand, the baron obliges Raoul to climb a terribly steep rock face while carrying her in his arms. On arriving at the top, the boy dies of exhaustion, and grief-stricken Mathilde throws herself into the void. Consumed with remorse, Mathilde's father builds a beautiful priory on the cursed summit, which still delights hikers today.

My 'territory' covers about five hundred hectares of forest. And I can say that I soon start finding my way around. First of all there are the paths followed by the animals, which I know by heart, and then a few special tricks that I develop with experience. Olfactory points of reference, first of all, are essential, particularly at night. It doesn't smell the same if I walk towards the grain fields situated towards the west, or if I walk towards the Seine. The oaks give off a scent of old wooden beams. Chestnuts, ferns, meadowsweet, all those smells help me find my bearings. If I approach a pond, for example, my nostrils catch the scent of rushes and mud. My eyes have also got used to the darkness. I don't yet have the eyesight of a cat, but my vision has already distinctly improved. Last of all there's touch. At night in the forest, you snooze, you go for a walk and you eat. But how to spot the good plants? Plantains and dock leaves, for example, look very similar, but I only have to touch the leaves to know which plant I'm dealing with: the ribs go in different directions. Obviously you don't acquire that level of knowledge after a weekend under the stars. It took me about two years to get there, and the forest still has plenty of secrets to reveal to me.

At this time of night, Daguet is bound to be in the spot where an ancient tree stands like the column of a cathedral in the middle of the young beeches. It's in a landscape bathed in light, where the golden rays of light ripple in long cascades and strike the forest, that I meet up with my friend. He is standing upright, he recognises me and continues looking at me. He looks proud, my prince of the forest, in spite of his spring moult, which gives him a slightly seedy appearance.

In the spring, as the days lengthen, the roe deer lose their winter fur to make way for their magnificent summer pelt. Their livery, that elegant tawny fleece that demands to be displayed properly, contains all the shades of red that give the fur a silky, polished appearance, while the gorget – the paler area on the throat – the rump patch and the underside assume a cream-coloured tone. Conversely, the autumn moult passes almost unnoticed. Within a few days, the fine summer coat is replaced by the winter coat. The fur thickens, and the brush of the does, in the middle of the rump patch, lengthens and becomes more obvious. In the males, the hairs around the penis sheath also lengthen.

Daguet seems a little stressed and worried to me, as if he is not quite himself. I sit down on the ground, cross-legged, my left buttock on the heel of my right shoe, and with my right buttock in the air so that I can switch buttocks after half an hour and prevent my legs from going numb. Such precision might seem pointless, but it's very important: you should never sit directly on the ground, because if the soil is damp all the layers of clothing you wear will absorb water, and it will be difficult to get them dry during the day. This will be followed in the night by a very unpleasant sensation of cold which does rather spoil the pleasure of being outdoors; more importantly, because of the ambient temperature, it could lead to chills or, worse, hypothermia. Daguet stands and waits. Suddenly he looks straight ahead of him and I recognise the face of Chocotte, a fine buck at least six years old who has been here a long time, even before I decided to explore the forest. He's a very likeable deer who, in spite of his age, his strong character and his impressive build, tends to run off if a pine cone falls to the ground a few metres away (much to the amusement of the squirrels). My young friend facing Chocotte lowers his head and presents his horny headdress. He shakes his head to make more of an impression on his adversary and scrapes the ground with his front hoof. Chocotte pretends to ignore the 'threat' represented by Daguet, and continues on his way as if the young buck doesn't exist. In any case he isn't interested in this patch of territory because he lives in the one opposite.

When two roe deer meet, they may sort out their differences by rubbing their heads against the trees and barking. At other times they resort to battle, head-to-head, but such battles are rare and the wounds minor. Having lived with these animals for seven years, I've never witnessed this kind of combat, which isn't to say that they don't fight. Like everywhere else, some individuals are more aggressive than others. At first, the battles look more like a game. That said, things can sometimes get serious. Sometimes the game degenerates and the aggressiveness of an individual can quickly mount thanks to a surge in testosterone. Territorial activity reaches a peak in May, and once the territorial perimeters have been established conflicts fade away, avoiding pointless demonstrations of strength.

In the background, behind Daguet, I notice another buck who is shyly coming forward. This is Brock, a very young and nervous buck who moves from territory to territory without being able to establish one for himself. He is among the less happy and more sensitive deer who, since they are unable to conquer a territory, seek refuge in little copses, thickets and even hedges, which makes their lives uncomfortable, not to say disastrous. These deer, with their difficult living conditions, are often young animals, less than three years old, or they may be very old deer, over the age of ten. Some never manage to obtain a range, whatever their age. Wounded, sick or too old, they can't compete and are liable to die, taking part in spite of themselves in the great circle of life and the self-regulation of the species. Each year other young deer, too weak or insufficiently combative to attract the attention of the older animals, are granted a second chance by their father, or by other older deer – a second year as 'protégés'. Later in the year, if something happens to their protector, they will temporarily assume their place and win the respect of their neighbours. They know the area, they have learned everything from their 'master', and if need be they can defend their territory against their adversaries, even those that are bigger and stronger than they are, at least until the following spring. As a rule, all the 'homeless' deer, whether male or female, are effectively banished from the well-located forests, and obliged to find precarious refuge, as well as poor-quality food, on open ground. Strangely, in the mountains and more particularly in the big coniferous forests of the Alps, I have observed that the roe deer in those locations do the opposite. They seek to live in the densest, darkest places, in the heart of the forests. That's where they survive, ready to come out as soon as an area is re-wooded (naturally or artificially). They thus move from the edge of the forest to the interior, while the stronger males occupy the territories on the forest rim.

Brock, seeking friendship and comfort, comes slowly forward towards Daguet who, seeing the weakness of his fellow, agrees to share a bit of territory with him. I'm obliged to leave my friend here and watch him move away with another new companion, because I'm concerned that this newcomer's jumpiness might break the trust that Daguet has granted me.

I notice that when my friend isn't there I'm on my own. So I decide to take lessons with deer other than Daguet, Six-Points, Star or Arrow, with the same technique; contrary to what you might think, it's not as easy as that. Just because Daguet trusts me and lets me walk behind him, it doesn't mean that the other deer who observe us will imitate him and trust me, too. It's more complicated than that, because this 'taming' work has to be repeated for each individual. Even in winter, when small groups form, if I have the trust of one deer I have to work with each of the other bucks and does separately in order to prove my good intentions, making use of the character of each. And my little roe deer do have different characters. Throughout the winter, the deer form groups that can include more than a dozen individuals, and sometimes they regroup, like their red deer cousins, but that doesn't mean that they live in herds. I go back in search of Six-Points, but he has left with Star for the chalky slopes beyond my territory. The bushes that grow there are very dense, and it's hard for me to penetrate them. So for now I abandon my attempt to go 'further' with them.

Buck + author stroll along together for a few hours

6

One evening I find Daguet, and we stroll along together for a few hours. On that spring night, with the buds on the trees taking their time to open and produce succulent fresh, sweet leaves, Daguet is hungry, and starts turning his nose up at the bramble leaves which, even though they have the advantage of being there all year round, develop a bitter taste as the winter drags on. We walk towards the edge of the forest, to a typical Norman farmhouse with a magnificent vegetable garden. Carrots, potatoes, leeks and beetroot grow here, near an orchard, beneath the envious eyes of the Norman cows that browse beneath the apple trees. Pretty flowers separate the furrows of vegetables, so that harmful insects don't destroy the crop. We cross a road which isn't very busy at that time of night, but it is as well to be cautious. In fact, since they constitute three-quarters of the hooved animals struck by the side of the road, many roe deer are sacrificed to road traffic. In the spring, the increased number of males is one of the reasons for this. The bucks also scatter to find new territories and, in the autumn, roe deer are disturbed by human activities such as hunting or excursions into the forest. Daguet leaps a chest-high wall and trots delightedly through the damp grass towards the vegetable garden. Here and there he plucks flowers covered with pretty pearls of dew. He lightly unearths the roots, devours a beetroot and a few beans, then returns to the forest at dawn before the farmer wakes up. The owner of the farm, accompanied by his dog, can't help but notice the results of this little nocturnal expedition into his garden. It's not vandalism, it's hunger; you have to learn to share, that's life in the country, and it's not as bad as wild boar. I've only known Daguet for a few months, and the rogue's already leading me off the straight and narrow. I'd have to say that I'm feeling pretty ravenous, too.

At this stage of the adventure, I'm still returning to civilisation every now and then, two or three times a month, to regain my strength. The processed foods that I find in the family fridge are still just as appetising as they were before, but I find them increasingly difficult to digest. Moving suddenly from my forest diet, one of bitter, harsh flavours, to the sweet/salt world of industrialised food, is a surprising experience. Fromage blanc – a soft white cheese – has a startling whiff of fungus. Industrial bread has never been so hard to chew, and hard-boiled eggs revolt me. I grab a few tins to complement the emergency supply that I accumulated at the start of my adventure. I recharge the batteries of my camera. To my despair, my solar charger has proved to be completely useless in the sunless depths of the forest. I also take a good hot shower. I sleep for a few hours in my childhood bed and leave before daybreak. I avoid my parents, who disapprove of my new man-of-the-woods lifestyle and have no qualms about saying so. Do I wash my clothes? No. I don't want to bring the smells of the world of human beings into the forest. It would make my roe deer friends extremely nervous. Apart from that, I've noticed that in the forest hygiene isn't a problem. I'll come back to that.

I'm still startled by the precision with which my friend Daguet and the other deer choose their food. With his ultra-mobile lips and delicate, long tongue, Daguet finds it easy to devour the wood anemones, hyacinths and several other plants that are supposed to be toxic to herbivores. He doesn't seem to be troubled by whatever substances they contain. It's because in his daily ration he seeks the precise amount of tannins he needs to balance his nutrition. His salivary glands, more particularly the parotids, make proteins that can destroy the toxins contained in these tannins. He has learned this food science from the very first month of his life as a fawn. His mother took him to feeding grounds where, by imitation, he learned to taste these particular plants in very small quantities. Now, thanks to his selectiveness and his extremely keen sense of smell, he quickly recognises the plants that give him what he needs and the ones that don't, without having to taste them. His liver, more highly developed in roe deer than in any other ruminant, inhibits the toxic substances secreted by plants to protect them from herbivores. On the other hand he has no gallbladder, so that a very particular process allows him to assimilate carbohydrates instantly in such a way that they reach his belly undamaged. Plants grown with fertiliser and replanted trees are more attractive to him than those grown naturally. The same is true of ornamental trees, new varieties of rose bush, ferns or tobacco plants, in short things that one is unlikely to come across in the forest. Let us state clearly that my happy band of friends love sweet, salt, bitter tastes and, as a rule, absolutely anything with a strong flavour. They are keen on woody and semi-woody plants with a high nutritional value. They can distinguish instantly between a plant bred in a greenhouse from one that has grown naturally. Brambles, ivy, heather, raspberries, haws and all the young leaves of the springtime trees are of great nutritional interest to them, provided, of course, that the tree is not too high, because being small the roe deer cannot reach food that it too high up. Beyond one metre twenty or so, the food will be eaten by the red deer, which is bigger than the roe. Tree trunks which were collar-cut the year before, and which have sprouted new shoots the following spring, are ideal. Much of the food that grows in the forest, such as brambles, oak leaves and the leaves of the acacia, wild cherries or wild plums, tastes bitter, harsh or of nothing at all.

We spend whole days in the undergrowth, waiting patiently for sunset so that we can leave for the glade, the meadow, the field or simply the edge of a path. You have to imagine the intense joy we feel when we dare to venture out into open ground to eat plantain, wild docks, dandelions and many

Daguet asleep. Nervous in appearance, roe deer are in fact peaceful animals that take time to enjoy life. One day I was sitting by a bramble bush along a path popular with walkers. Suddenly I heard snoring coming from the depths of the thicket. It was Daguet: he was sound asleep, untroubled by people passing.

other succulent plants, sweet or starchy, salty or spicy. With roe deer, you don't live *in* the forest but *of* the forest; it's a subtle but important difference. On the other hand, during the cold season, less food is available and the bulk of their food comes from brambles. To adapt to the nutritional constraints of the forest, roe deer have had to adjust several times during their evolution. Their first ancestors, which appeared twenty-five million years ago, had very highly developed canines in their upper jaws. With the gradual disappearance of large fruit trees due to the climate change at the time, roe deer evolved towards their current form during the Middle Pleistocene, two hundred thousand years ago, and the structure of their ankle bones suggests to palaeontologists that they appeared long before red deer or fallow deer. Unlike other cervids, which need to consume a very large amount of herbaceous vegetable food with a low nutritional value, roe deer have preferred to forage selectively, finding their food more easily on trees or bushes. That's why I call my companions gourmet gleaners, selecting their food for its high nutritional value and choosing the best they can find. If leaves, buds, berries and the year's young shoots are part of their range of varied tastes, fruits are also highly appreciated. Without knowing it, my friends play an ecological role, by dispersing certain seeds, like those of the sorb apple tree, which germinate in their digestive tracts. On the other hand, they eat grass only rarely, because it is not rich enough in nutrients for them to survive. As the species evolved, the incisors in the upper jaw were replaced by a little cushion of cartilage, a roll that bumps against the teeth of the lower jaw when the mouth is closed. They draw woody twigs deep into their mouths to chew them with their molars rather than sever them with their incisors as rodents do. A roe deer that lives in the forest, even an old one, will have incisors that are much less worn down than the roe deer of the plains, because there is more food of better quality in the forest, and the twigs tend to be more tender. A roe deer's stomach, composed of the rumen, the reticulum, the omasum and the abomasum, is so small (about five litres) that Daguet is obliged to eat very regularly, ten to fifteen times a day. After eating, when he is sated, he likes to chew the cud calmly under cover, or perhaps in the open if he feels safe. I can tell from his expression that this is a moment of pure relaxation for him. That isn't to say that he stops observing his surroundings, his ears detecting the slightest noise or his nostrils discerning the slightest scent. In order to digest their food, roe deer need calm, and intrusions (a herd of red deer, a group of boar or some passing humans) have a direct influence on eating times. These untimely irruptions can put the deer in a state of extreme distress, and if this is repeated too often the deer become fearful, are startled by the slightest noise, and in some cases can find themselves in a real 'state of hysterics'. Food must be taken regularly throughout the day, but also at night. With experience, the deer learn to keep a low profile, and when they are bothered too frequently, for example at dawn or dusk, they can alter their daily routine to eat in the middle of the day so as not to be disturbed at an important moment.

Back in the woods, and after a good hour's rest, we pass through a recently planted part of the forest. In a monotonous, rectilinear landscape we eat by gleaning the tender leaves of young plants. Oak, ash, wild cherries, all of great interest to foresters, seem to attract the special attention of my little Daguet. It's budding time, and the buds themselves are a source of endless pleasure. We're like kids in a sweetshop, faced with delicacies each tastier than the last. Sometimes he eats the end bud of the plant. Those terminal buds are no more appetising than the lateral ones, but you need to look ahead, because those young trees aren't going to be small all their lives, so they have to be preserved to ensure a perennial abundance of food. Roe deer are in a sense the gardeners of the forest who maintain the vegetation. This browsing does not lead to the death of the plants, but adapts the growth of the tree, which sometimes assumes a bushy shape with multiple bifurcations. For foresters, these trees have no value; they are 'economically' dead. But nature works differently, with each individual responding to stimuli and defending itself as best it can. Life always finds a way and you need to trust in it. Corsican pines and spruces planted in the middle of the forest are of no interest to Daguet, at least not from a nutritional point of view. But they may be of use to us this winter in case of scarcity.

We gradually leave this patch of woodland and climb a little path lined with random growths of buckthorn and birches. After eating a good quantity of vegetation, we look for a place to chew the cud in peace. We are heading towards the territory of Harry, a very powerful roe deer. Like Six-Points, Harry becomes quite frightening during the territorial marking period, and I'm a bit worried about my insouciant friend. I walk behind Daguet and the more I observe his gait, the more he seems to be going askew. He seems to be in a very curious state and looks a little agitated. Because he's making a lot of noise, grunting for no reason, even going so far as barking on Harry's territory, it won't be long before Harry replies. I spot the outline of this impressive deer; he's big and muscular, with huge antlers. Daguet advances very confidently, almost nonchalantly, towards the strongest and most territorial roe deer in the area. He trips along gaily, and

Harry looks intrigued. All of a sudden he barks very loudly in the direction of Daguet, who freezes for a moment and turns towards Harry with an idiotic expression, as if to say, 'Have you lost your mind? You scared me there!' Harry furiously charges Daguet, who continues to act strangely. He stops a few centimetres away from him. Disturbed and surprised, Harry recoils slightly and then charges again. Daguet takes a blow to the side, falls and whines a little but then gets up again as if nothing has happened. Caught off guard, the bigger, stronger deer is alarmed, moves away a little and barks at the top of his voice. Daguet approaches me and hides just behind me. I'm not too happy about this, because if Harry charges again I wouldn't want to be caught between the two of them. But in the end Harry leaves, barking, very disgruntled. He's bound to come back this evening to mark his territory again. We set off for Daguet's home range again. Looking slightly distraught, he comes and stands against a tree on the edge of a clearing. He leans against the trunk and looks at me. In fact, he has no choice: he has to wait for it to pass. Because Daguet is, quite simply, drunk. In the autumn, the plants concentrate large quantities of alkaloids, saponoids and polyphenols in their cells as well as other substances that will enable them to protect the buds and resist the big winter frosts. They manufacture a kind of anti-freeze which, when ingested by roe deer, has the same effect as strong alcohol, hence the occasional amusing sight of animals tottering down forest avenues. A few years ago, in my *département* of the Eure, a roe deer living near the little town of Bourgtheroulde-Infreville took up residence under the kitchen table of a hotel restaurant and refused to leave; it took ages to dislodge it. Since the quantity of these substances varies from one plant to another, it doesn't affect all roe deer, only the greediest ones.

7

In the early morning I'm filled with an inexplicable sense of joy. Daguet is taming me more and more, and even comes over to my feet to sniff the scent of my shoes. He observes my behaviour, while remaining very vigilant at all times. I notice that he mostly looks at my hands when he approaches, probably out of fear that they might grab him. But I press my arms against my body and present the palms of my hands so that he can smell them. That reassures him, and he can see that I don't move. I don't even try and stroke him, though God knows it's tempting. We walk to the pine grove where Six-Points is master. I don't know if it's a provocation, but Daguet seems sure that he wants to go in there. It's very early, and very dark. The day is struggling to break through the ambient gloom when some little noises like whispering can be heard. Daguet, with his extraordinary sense of hearing, picks them up immediately and sets off, probably to discover where they're coming from. We move cautiously forward. He stops regularly, sniffs the surrounding air and seems intrigued. It isn't fear but curiosity. Suddenly, a few metres away, I can just make out Star in the darkness. She's alone and lying down, and Six-Points isn't beside her. When she notices Daguet she sniffs in our direction, rises breathlessly to her feet and struggles towards us, barking faintly. Daguet retreats with a series of little hops. I'm ready to follow him but I'm worried about Star, who doesn't seem to me to be in the best shape. I let my friend leave, so that I can stay and observe Star for a moment.

It's very cold for June this morning. Star has seen me and recognised my scent. For a few weeks I've gained some trust from Six-Points, but even more from Star, who seems intrigued by my presence. She's an experienced doe and, even though we haven't been through anything exceptional together, her curiosity goes beyond our respective encounters. I have deep respect for this very intelligent little female. She doesn't say anything to me, lies down again about ten metres away and then stares at me for a few long minutes before settling down to sleep for a while. At least that's what I think she's doing. I don't move, and that's the right thing to do, because a few moments later I see her gently opening her eyes, still staring in my direction. It was a trick to see if I would approach her, thinking she was asleep. When you play with roe deer, you must never imagine you're smarter than they are. You're bound to come out worse.

A few moments later, visibly weakened, she struggles to her feet, her whole body trembling, as if she's about to collapse like a house of cards. She takes a step forward and then stops.

I pray with all my heart that there isn't something seriously wrong with her. I see a thin trickle of fluid emerging from her hindquarters. She utters some little groans and I see that she's making an incredible effort to contain the pain she feels. I take a few steps to the side to gain a better view of her pale rump, when I realise that the greatest gift that life can give us is taking place before my very eyes. She's giving birth. The pains were only contractions, and I'm witnessing the birth of some little fawns that are having trouble coming out. I think that's why Six-Points isn't around. As a rule, female roe deer don't like males to be roaming about the territory when pregnancy comes to term. Two trembling hoofs which have pierced the placenta dangle stiffly into the void. I'm so happy and so close to Star that I'm almost tempted to go and help her deliver them. But common sense tells me not to, and I allow her that moment of intimacy. I share her pain, and with each little groan she utters I am aware of the immense effort the brave little doe is making. First contraction, nothing. Second contraction, still nothing. She pushes again and the effort is intense. Minutes pass, another contraction, then another, when, all of a sudden, out comes the young fawn, falling to the ground with a noise proportionate to its weight: bam! There he is, welcome to the earth, little one.

Deep within me I feel a joy as immense as if I had brought him into the world myself. I also feel pride for my little doe who, alone in the face of pain, was able to get through this trial. I wait for a second fawn, but there isn't going to be anything more. There's only one, he's a little male and I call him

Chévi. Star takes a few moments to recover herself, and then turns to her fawn. Chévi's whole body is quivering. She licks him to dry him, but also to establish the bond that will unite them in the future. She finishes eating the placenta that is still stuck to him in places and which, if it happened to be discovered by a fox or another predator, could endanger both the newborn, who can't yet walk, and the mother, left very much weakened by this little tot, ruffled as he is by the rough licking of his mother's tongue. After an hour, this lad tries to stand up by himself. The first attempt fails. The second go works, but he falls after a few seconds and immediately gets up again and takes three steps before stumbling into the weeds. Exhausted by the effort of being born, the little fawn collapses with exhaustion, huddled against his loving mother.

A little while later, Chévi gets up again, more confidently this time, makes his way towards one of the four teats and starts pulling ravenously on them. His mother will feed him from the breast for five months. Lying beside him, she also seems to want to go to sleep. She licks him all over one last time, runs her tongue affectionately over his muzzle and then turns her head towards me. Plainly surprised, she stares at me for a long time. With all her efforts, she must have forgotten that I was there. I turn around very slowly and then, as delicately as I can, I go back to see Daguet, my heart light and my head still spinning from all the emotion. She watches me go. I know that Chévi will spend his first few weeks hidden in the undergrowth and then, once he's a little stronger, he will walk behind his mother. In the meantime, I have to leave him in peace, because even though Star knows me well I don't know how she would react if my scent mixed with that of her little one. So I prefer not to take any risks, and to leave him in peace. I've already got Daguet, Arrow, a few other acquaintances, and then, with Six-Points, I may also have the privilege of bumping into Chévi trotting behind his mother.

For a female roe deer, giving birth isn't much fun. Births are staggered and in some cases several hours can pass between the arrival of the first fawn and that of the second. The intense effort involved in giving birth weakens the mother, and if one of the young is in an unusual position she may not survive. That means three deaths all at once, because the little fawns will not be suckled by their mother and will die only a few hours later. Sadly, such deaths occur frequently, because the does are naturally predisposed to give birth to their young in different places. In that case the newborn may potentially fall victim to a roaming predator, or even die of cold if its mother does not come back very soon. The first six months are crucial for the fawns' survival. The mortality rate is higher during the first month of their life, regardless of sex, and goes unnoticed by humans. Does younger than two years old are not yet physically mature enough to have young. They do not reproduce, or only rarely, they weigh less than twenty kilos and very seldom come into heat. Star has only one fawn because she is young and light, and does indeed appear to weigh only about twenty kilos. Observing my different doe friends, I note that the number of fawns that a doe can carry is strongly linked to her weight. The lighter she is, the fewer the number of offspring she will have. I happen to know that a doe in a neighbouring forest (Lyons-la-Forêt), where food is abundant, has had triplets, but her weight is close to thirty kilos. That phenomenon has to do with the self-regulation of the species in the absence of predators. In fact the fluctuation of births is intrinsically linked to the availability of food supplies at the time of conception. Some females like Magnolia, whom we will meet later, do not have a very highly developed maternal instinct, and many of them lose their entire litter, while others, who are more devoted and have a dominant character, manage to conquer a high-quality home range with a rich supply of food for themselves and their offspring. That leads to very rich milk for the sturdy young fawns. Since the deer do not change partners, character traits persist and each year the same scene tends to repeat itself, which can shape the continued existence of an entire line.

As with all the other fawns, Chévi's first days on earth are lived out in the undergrowth, where the doe knows that it is safe, and where it can develop its strength. It's also that first week that determines the maximum physical growth of all the fawns. Once past that critical phase, it will be able to follow its mother almost everywhere with great agility. And to defend her young, like all the other does in the forest, Star demonstrates unflagging devotion. In fact, mothers have no hesitation in flicking vipers away, chasing off foxes and, in the most extreme cases, they can stand as an obstacle in a hunter's line of fire. In spite of this, the rate of death due to natural predators remains significant, particularly in early summer, but also during the winter when the layer of snow hinders the movement of the young fawns from one place to another, making them more vulnerable than the adults. Meanwhile, during that first week, when she sets off in search of food, Star puts Chévi in a safe place, 'ordering' him, with a little cry, to lie there until she gets back. She can leave him alone for several hours. Luckily, Chévi's coat acts as an effective camouflage, a pattern of white patches on a brownish background. These markings will fade very quickly over the course of July, perhaps even from the first weeks after his birth. In August the initial pattern of patches will only be very faintly visible, making way by the end of September for a thick winter coat similar in every respect to that of the adults. His throat will also be decorated by the white patch known as a gorget.

My day continues beside Daguet, but I can't help thinking about that little fawn, so small and so frail, now living not far from me (this is the only time that I will ever witness a birth). The images keep running through my head. I'm sorry not to have had my camera with me at that moment, because I would have loved to immortalise those fine moments. I don't even have a photograph of Star from those days. My mind is so far away that I end up losing sight of Daguet, who was walking ahead of me and plainly didn't want to wait. A storm is brewing. I don't think it's going to be a violent one, but I'd still like to get back under the pines that give shelter from the wind. I sit down. An hour later I spot Six-Points, who doesn't yet know that he's a father. I try to follow him and he joins in with the game to a certain extent, but it's always complicated with

Six-Points. In spite of our years of living close to one another, even though he is well aware that I wish him no harm, and even though he happily accepts my presence when I walk behind him, I still have a sense that his head has somehow understood but his body remains reticent. That gives him a curious gait – his front hooves are quite relaxed, in harmony with his head, while his stiff hindquarters seem to want to go faster and faster, as if trying to overtake his whole body. I put myself at a greater distance so as not to alarm him. In this kind of exercise you mustn't impose, just suggest. It's his choice. I talk to him, I tell him how much I'd like to stroke and caress him and share a moment of his life. I'm sure that my tone of voice reassures him, and that it plays a major part in his acceptance of me. I let him finish marking his territory, move further away and disappear. For now I'm going to settle in for the night before it rains, prepare my 'mattress' by breaking off some fir-tree branches and rest for a moment. That'll do me good after such an emotional day. Let's take advantage of it being summer.

He speaks to the Deer using a soft tone of voice

8

Summer is well advanced, and I'm honoured by the growing trust that Daguet places in me. It's warm, the sky is deep blue and the sun is blazing. The mornings are still damp, and to warm himself up a little Daguet decides to go and lie down in the tall weeds of a glade that I call 'the fox's clearing'. It was there, at the age of fourteen, that I photographed the first doe of my life. A few weeks later I thought I might be able to see it again. But a fine black fox had taken up residence in a burrow not far away, and had probably put my doe off the idea of going for a stroll. It was also the end of spring, and if she was expecting young, she certainly wouldn't have wanted to risk venturing into that area. Daguet nibbles some grass, and while he does that I 'borrow' some melons and watermelons that the hunters have left at the foot of the young apple trees whose trunks are protected by wooden pickets and chicken wire. These 'treats' aren't meant for me, but I'm sure the boar won't be angry with me for pilfering their offerings; and then I also reckon that they're quite fat enough already.

Portrait of Chévi. Roe deer are unguligrades, they walk on their hooves, which are as sharp as a razor. Once Chévi, to give me a cuddle, trod on my shoes in order to reach my face. His hoof went right through my shoe and injured my foot.

*lying down together in a
clearing the deer then
presses his body against him*

Deer Man   65

My belly full of fruit, I lie down in the clearing. Daguet joins
me and the strangest thing happens: he comes and presses
himself against me, looking at me with a sated and trusting
expression. I feel his warm body against my leg. He curls up
with his head on my knee and rests. I have an overwhelming
desire to put my hand on his fur to stroke him, but I'm worried that he might not appreciate that, and that it would put
him off getting close to me. A moment later he lifts his head
slightly, yawns, looking at me, and then lowers it again and
rests it against my thigh, near my hand. I take advantage of
this to stroke his cheek a little with my thumb. He seems to
like that. I withdraw my hand gently to put it on his back. I
stroke him for a long time, observing his reactions. He relaxes
and closes his eyes. Sometimes his muscles tremble slightly,
but then you have to remember that this is an animal that has
no idea what a human caress is, so it's a completely normal
response. I'm trembling a little, too, because it's a first for me
as well. The muscular tension eases as I stroke him and in the
end he falls asleep peacefully. From time to time he groans
a little, grunts or twitches his hoofs slightly. He is clearly
dreaming. He's sleeping deeply, because I feel the weight
of his body getting increasingly heavy against me. The roe
deer is not an animal known for its liking of close contact.
Nonetheless, when two individuals are fond of each other it is
not unknown for them to groom one another. Demonstrations
of affection can even be repeated at any time during the year,
but especially during the mating season, when such gestures
become more frequent since they are part of the courtship

*He begins to stroke the
Deer & is accepted*

ritual. At any rate, my friend seems to enjoy my caresses, and I am delighted to provide them.

So we take advantage of this peaceful morning; the bees spin around above our heads and gather pollen from the few flowers scattered around the meadow. Not a sound disturbs the fullness of the moment. I use the time to study the horizon for a while, because deep in the forest you can never see further than twenty or thirty metres. It feels good to 'breathe'. Suddenly, in the distance, I spot some walkers. They are coming in our direction, but I don't pay them any particular attention. They're on a hiking path, and we are hidden by the tall grass. Moments later I become aware that they're cutting across the meadow where we are sitting, heading straight towards us while Daguet is still peacefully asleep. They are level with us now. A man and a woman in their fifties, walking at a steady pace, without a word, without a sound, sticks in hand. Daguet is still asleep. I am preparing to get abruptly to my feet, as soon as Daguet becomes aware of the suspicious scent or opens an eyelid at the sound of the people passing, but nothing happens, absolutely nothing. He's out for the count. The two walkers say hello as they pass, and I reply. They smile and continue on their way. I can't get over it. On my lap I have a roe deer that I'm stroking – Daguet, who doesn't move so much as a hair, he feels so much at ease against me – and the walkers must have thought it was my dog. I'm blown away.

A quarter of an hour later, my sleeping beauty wakes like a flower. He studies the landscape for a moment, runs a tongue over his muzzle, sniffs the air and gets to his feet. He stretches his whole body, snorts, and then licks his fur as if nothing has happened. Apparently for him nothing has happened. I imagine that he feels he can trust me, and that he's been able to relax a little, sleep without worrying about anything, set aside his vigilance by trusting a friend, and abandon for a few moments the heavy burden of simply being alive.

It's an honour for me, my friend, to keep watch over you.

The deer feels complete trust.

9

Daguet and I leave the clearing to go deeper into the forest. While he eats some blackberries on the edge of the wood, I move away as discreetly as possible to keep him from following me, and edge in the direction of Six-Points' territory. To avoid any misunderstanding, I always try to make sure that Daguet and Six-Points don't bump into each other. At a bend in a path I come across Star, who is followed by Chévi, and it occurs to me that this would be a good opportunity to let this little fawn tame me. Chévi was born three months ago, he has now been weaned and he will go on learning from his mother until the end of the winter. He's in great shape and that reassures me, because living in a hostile environment calls for a certain sturdiness. Many fawns don't make it through the first year. Anything can happen in the forest. Internal parasites, such as lungworm or liver fluke, and external parasites, such as sucking lice, nasal botflies, deer keds, and in some rare cases warble fly, or even just a very damp period of cold weather, can weaken the young deer's health and sometimes lead to death. Of course, the discovery of these lifeless little bodies always fills me with sadness. That said, however, mortality has to be seen as a natural regulation of space that preserves the balance of the woodland, if we allow nature to fulfil its work without ever intervening.

With Chévi, the few times that our paths have crossed I have never attempted an approach. It's too dangerous for him, because he could still mistake my scent for that of his mother, and she would probably abandon him. I think that being tamed by Chévi is going to be a lot of fun. His mother trusts me, his father knows me very well, and since he's a young animal with no preformed ideas about the world, he won't mind me approaching him. What a fantasy. I move towards Star, who trusts me. She doesn't say anything to me. Chévi is lying quite close by, calm and serene. He observes everything, he's intrigued by everything but not threatened, because he still – or at least this is what I think – still trusts his mother implicitly. I approach very gently and sit down a few metres in front of him. He stares at me, ears pricked and pointed in my direction, furtively glancing at his mother to observe her reactions, but she still doesn't respond, doesn't even look at us. With his big hypersensitive ears turning independently in all directions, he reacts to the slightest suspicious or unfamiliar sound, and is immediately vigilant. With time he will learn to tell the difference between familiar and dangerous sounds. The noise of a tractor, for example, or the wailing of a chain-saw as it cuts down the trees, will be classed as 'innocent',

The scent of anemones. Highly poisonous to other herbivores, wood anemones are eaten in large quantities by roe deer in the spring. Since they have no gallbladder, the toxin has no effect on them apart from preventing certain illnesses.

because they are part of his daily auditory experiences, while the crack of a twig when everything is otherwise silent will inevitably put him on full alert.

Chévi sniffs the air and seems to be startled, because he gets up quickly to join his mother. The hairs on his pale rump patch bristle with his growing alarm. In fact, the contraction of the subcutaneous muscles around the hairs on his rear form an alarm signal of immaculate whiteness, and allow a family to stay safe as a group; a pursuing predator will see a pretty white patch plunging into the forest until the deer turns off to the side and ... the white patch is gone. An excellent diversion. At the same time the scent glands send a substance into the air to warn the other deer moving around nearby of imminent danger. I walk quite a long way behind him, because he trots swiftly and goes skipping off in all directions. Every now and again Star turns to see what the fuss is all about, looks at us and then sets off again. Chévi presses against his mother's leg as if he is in mortal danger, whines faintly and glances regularly at her as if to say: 'Don't you see that big, strange thing that's been following us for the last few moments?' Even if Star doesn't seem to pay much attention to his concerns (she knows I'm not dangerous), Chévi emits such anxiety that he communicates some of it to his mother, who is now becoming a bit nervous. I notice that Chévi has an instinctive fear of humans and other animals such as boar and squirrels. Nothing will make him change his mind, not even his mother, or perhaps it will take some time before he works out that I'm harmless.

A moment later, when I'm walking alongside Star and not intending to go anywhere near Chévi (I'd lost sight of him, in fact), he sets off at the speed of a bullet. Without thinking, Star runs after him, thinking perhaps that he's fleeing some kind of threat. I don't stop to think either, and go after her. When we get close to Chévi, he sets off again at top speed. Star follows him again and I do the same. It's utterly baffling. There's nothing, absolutely no danger of any kind. Everything is calm and peaceful. The little game is resumed three or four times and Star becomes anxious. The more we run, the more stressed Chévi becomes, the greater his mother's anxiety, and we have all become palpably nervous. Then I let him run some distance away in order to ease the tension. He stops, waits for his mother, and calms down. I let them both leave without pressing matters, because I don't want to exhaust him for no good reason or create a mental barrier that would later prevent him from living with me. I realise that fawns, even very young ones, only trust their mothers for the first few weeks, and that their individualism and their 'free will' increase as they grow. Chévi isn't content with imitating his mother; he learns to listen and observe, guided by his own instinct. He sees that his mother trusts me, but he can't understand it for now and it frightens him. He hasn't yet analysed the different postures that I can adopt in front of him, because unlike his elders he has no experience of other humans, whether runners, walkers, hunters or woodsmen, with whom to make comparisons. His survival instinct takes the upper hand and, overcome with emotion, he takes flight. So I abandon the idea of making friends with him, because he is too 'wild' for now. With time, perhaps he will accept me as his father and mother already do. We'll see.

10

Autumn has settled over the forest and adorned the leaves of the trees with a thousand colours, from pale yellow to dark red. When this season arrives, I always like to bring to mind the Native American legend of the Huron-Wyandot, who gave the roe deer the divine name of Dehenyanteh, which means 'he for whom the rainbow has made a path of colours'.*

Envious of the Little Turtle, the guardian of the sky, the Deer wanted to leave the Great Island and, more than anything, wanted to have access to the big blue sky. To fulfil his ambition, he consulted the Thunder God, who advised

---

* According to *Les Hurons-Wendats: Une civilisation méconnue*, Georges E. Sioui, Presses Université Laval, 1994, and William E. Connelley, 'Religious Conceptions of the Modern Hurons', *The Mississippi Valley Historical Review*, Oxford University Press, on behalf of the Organization of American Historians, 1922.

him to climb into the sky using a rainbow. Then the Deer waited for the spring and, after the first rain sent by the Thunder God, he took the path traced by the rainbow. He quickly found himself in the sky, where he was free to run as he wished. At the same time, having met in council, the animals looked for the deer. The Wolf searched the woods, while the Hawk studied the sky. It was then that they all saw the Deer gambolling with great agility. The animals decided to go to the sky via the bridge of all the colours. The Bear reproached the deer for thinking only of himself and forgetting all the other animals on the Great Island. Defying his rebukes, the Deer provoked the Bear into a duel. The battle commenced straight away. Swift as lightning, the Deer stabbed the Bear with his pointed antlers. The Bear was mortally injured and the blood flowed abundantly from his wounds. The blood flowed all the way to the Great Island, where the leaves of the trees were coloured by the animal's blood. Since then, each year, when autumn returns, nature commemorates the battle of the Deer and the Bear, and the leaves of the trees turn red.

According to tradition, the beauties of autumn when nature dies are a source of nostalgia for the souls of the departed remembering their old terrestrial home. Even the gods return to live in the Great Island, because autumn is a time for the spirit. During this season the Pleiades, the most beautiful of the stars, leave their celestial home to come and live in the sky of the Great Island.

In the meantime, the equinoxes have passed and, as the season advances, the nights grow longer until the winter solstice comes. In the cool morning I nibble on chestnuts that I roasted over a wood fire the previous evening. I have enough of them to eat whenever I want, as snacks. You can't leave them too long, however, because there's a risk of them rotting, given the week-long damp. I dried the last ones on a bed of embers that I'm going to go on feeding for several days. After that I'll seal them in a hermetic bag to keep them for later.

Getting through the winter requires rigour. The most important thing is to come up with solutions to fight the cold at any time of day or night, anywhere in the forest. I only know one way of doing that: keep little supplies of dead wood, made up of twigs, fir branches, tree bark and pine cones, and store them around the place. As for food, I now have a good knowledge of the area. Even in the depths of winter you can find enough to live on: roots, tubers, wild carrots. To ensure a supply of protein I make stores of hazelnuts.

Sadly, even though I still hope I'll be able to do without it one day, I still feel the need to stay in contact with the world of humans. Every now and then I go home, or, rather, to my parents' house, to stock up on calories and get warm again. But for several months I've had a strange sensation when putting my feet on concrete floors. They're hard, cold and perfectly flat. I'm not used to them any more. I eat a bowl of fromage blanc with cereal and a lot of sugar. While I'm recharging my camera batteries, I'm assailed by smells. The smell of the

Mist. Winter isn't the most difficult season. The body gets used to the cold. On the other hand the frequent rain in spring and autumn forced me to pay particular attention to my clothes. When they were wet, I wrung them out and then blew air into them so that the fibres would swell and become watertight again.

fridge, the smell of bleach, of heating, of carpet, of clothes, clean or dirty, even the smell of the people who live in the house. Before setting off again I always slip a few bags of pasta into my bag, along with some tins of tuna and sardines. Last of all, I sometimes go to a shop to buy the two items that are indispensable for my survival: sealable bags for storing food and matches to make a fire.

I like to go walking at dawn and enjoy the sunrise when I can see it. But there's a frost this morning, and the clouds are piling up at the bottom of the valley. From the field where I'm standing I can just make out the belltower of the church in the village below. The grass is cool and the passing cows seem to enjoy this food, with its monotonous flavour. I lean against a barbed wire fence, on which some magnificent garden spiders have spun webs that are now pearled with dew. I feel good here, watching the world wake up. Young rabbits chase one another and then race against their mother. Three or four of them try and tip her over to get at the teats from which she probably stopped feeding them ages ago. A badger comes up the pebbly path, grunting and panting. I'm reassured to see him like that, because by nature badgers are always gruff and apparently dissatisfied, but most particularly because the road at the bottom of the valley is particularly dangerous for them, and I always hope they'll make it back alive from their little outing. It's a shame to get flattened after a good night's hunting by a driver in a hurry to get to work. The chaffinches aren't really singing this morning, they're whistling the song of the coming rain. I find their song so sad for birds that are usually so cheerful! And the blue tits imitating them – it's depressing!

The fog thickens, and it's hard to make out the edge of the forest. I spot a black fox, a vixen that I know every well, having encountered her several times with Daguet. I call her Terylle. She's magnificent. Her chest is a sumptuous white that contrasts with her little greyish paws. Her brush, always aligned with her body, is majestically voluptuous. She's really a beautiful fox. She walks along the fence that lines the forest, stops for a moment and seems to think. I don't move, because I don't want her to see me. I prefer to observe her 'in her natural state'. She sniffs the air in all directions, lowers her head and starts crossing the field, then freezes and looks at the cows. Given her size, they have nothing to fear and neither do their calves. She approaches the first cow, which tries to give her a little kick with a hind hoof as she passes. She makes her way towards the next. I'm intrigued by her little game. One cow, lying down and drowsing, doesn't seem to pay any attention to Terylle, who approaches gently. She doesn't chase the fox away, as her attitude isn't threatening. She sits down in front of the cow and observes it. The cow gives the fox a slightly stupid look and continues to chew the cud with its eyes half closed. Terylle takes a little step forward, then another, and quickly recoils. She starts again. One small step, then another, and a jump backwards. She repeats this little game several times. Each time she carefully studies the reactions of the cow, which still isn't moving an inch. Then she approaches the swollen teats and starts licking the milk that is seeping from them, with no reaction from the cow. Terylle stops for a moment and darts a fearful look at the cow, still without the slightest reaction.

I'm dumbfounded. A vixen has just shown me something I should have thought of a long time ago: drinking milk. Sated, Terylle strides off into the mist. I slip in turn among the herd to try and find a cow that won't mind me approaching her, without getting kicked on the nose. I see one that might be agreeable. I squat down in front of her and start milking. Her udder is full to the brim, and the veins feeding it are enormous. It occurs to me that I'm going to bring her some relief. It will do us both good. What joy. What pleasure to feel the lukewarm milk flowing down my throat. It's fat and thick and naturally sweet, and I'm delighted by this moment spent in the company of the cows.

Drinking is one of the most intense pleasures when you live in a forest, because drinking water is never available in large quantities. The hardest thing isn't finding it, because the plants that I eat in the morning and the evening are covered with dew, and their leaves largely consist of water. I'm drinking and eating at the same time, you might say. And that's the reason why roe deer can drink up to three litres of water a day without going to a water source. But our consumer society has accustomed us to drinking a certain quantity of liquid by the glass or the bottle. So when you no longer have access to that sensation of having drunk, the feeling of dehydration can become frankly disagreeable. To slake my thirst, there are two solutions: the first, after rain, is to use a sock to filter the water that has accumulated in a witch's well – those little natural cavities formed in trees when they grow into two or three trunks – they are often found in beechwoods. Once it's been filtered, I just have to put it in my billycan and boil it on a little wood fire. The second solution is to go two and a half kilometres west of my territory. There's a little Veolia reservoir station there, called Wolf Valley, not very secure, and with an outside tap. It's mostly used by inspectors to check its potability. It's unofficially free to use, behind a fence damaged by the woods and the weather. I just have to slip underneath to get to it and fill my two water bottles with cold water. Well, now I've discovered a third way of slaking my thirst. And it's with a bellyful of milk that I set off in search of Daguet, to continue this day that has begun so well.

By this stage of the story you're probably wondering how I address issues of hygiene. Well, first of all, I have one considerable advantage: I barely grow a beard. Regular washing of my feet, armpits and genitals is quite enough. But if I struggle to find things to drink, what trick have I put in place to wash myself? Well, right in the middle of the forest there's a remarkable tree called the Four Brothers. Four magnificent beeches, forty metres high, that probably sprouted from a fallen tree, and which have grown perfectly symmetrically, like quadruplets, forming at their centre a big cauldron that acts as a perfect collecting point for rainwater. That store of water is pretty much enough for me to wash in. And you're probably wondering what I look like. For the first few months, the insects wouldn't leave me in peace: I was bitten everywhere.

But over time the skin hardens and thickens, and resistance to the cold improves. The result is that my skin is in great condition. As to my dental hygiene, it's no longer a problem because I no longer eat sugar. I run my index finger over my teeth with a mixture of water and ash and the job's done. Obviously this little cocktail doesn't taste like supermarket toothpaste, but compared to the flavours of my diet since the start of this adventure, there's nothing really shocking about that.

11

One interminable autumn night, I've been walking with Star for a few hours. She's on her own, and she has probably left Chévi somewhere in the beech forest with Six-Points and Daguet, who have formed a winter friendship, and in whose company I have spent the last three days. It's cold in the early light, and the undergrowth is covered with a thick layer of mist. The morning silence isn't troubled by a breath of wind. In the plantation currently under development, the brambles have been crushed by tractors and we struggle to find a place where food hasn't been replaced by mud. The ground is slippery everywhere, and several times I nearly fall into the ruts left by the tyres. It's been raining constantly for several days, causing ponds to overflow and soak the ground. It's harder and harder to keep going without sinking into the ground with every step.

We continue our walk into the pine forest where it's less damp, and that's where we spend the afternoon. Star eats some chanterelles, and I take the rest and put the mushrooms in the bottom of my billycan. My plan is to cook them over a wood fire this evening. I'm soaked, I'm cold, and a good hot meal with soup made from old nettles and bramble leaves with mushrooms will do me the world of good. The little fire will also dry my clothes, which need it. Star moves along a steep path at the bottom of which a woodcutting path separates the pinewood from the oak forest. I hold back a little, because I know the way and, more importantly, I know that she's so cautious that it will take her several hours of reflection before she crosses the road, so I wait behind and pick mushrooms.

Jimmy. Jimmy, a boar, was a fabulous friend; he weighed almost a hundred kilos. Trapped together during a shoot, we made friends. Gobette, his companion, had had one foot torn off by a bullet and almost all of her boarlets had been killed. Since then, whenever he saw hunters, Jimmy had no hesitation in charging at them.

Then all of a sudden something strange vibrates under my feet. I don't know what it is, I've never felt anything like it. An earthquake? In Normandy? Impossible. All of a sudden a gunshot rips through the silence of the forest. I immediately look around for Star. Panicking, she is climbing the ridge of the narrow valley that overlooks the forest path to try and assess the situation and work out where the noise is coming from. The ground under my feet goes on vibrating more and more intensely, when I see about twenty red deer, stags and does, charging towards me in a disorderly gallop. I manage to hide behind a tree and narrowly avoid a collision with a running doe. At last the crazed herd disappears into the distance. In one brief and dizzying moment a second rifle shot rings out and a bullet grazes Star. She starts running again, dashes past me, barking to signal the imminent danger to the others: 'Baaah! . . . Baaah! . . . Bah, bah, bah!' She runs with all her might. My blood freezes, and I drop my billycan and run after her through the pinewood. I struggle to follow her, because the trees are densely packed together, and there are so many branches on the ground that it is hard to run while also looking ahead. Finally, a few seconds later, she slows down. I see her tottering slightly. I run breathlessly over to her and try to gauge the seriousness of her wound, without being able to find it. In the distance I hear four blasts on a hunting horn – the signal for roe deer. The hunting hounds, recognisable by the bells around their necks and the loud rattle they make, spread terror through the undergrowth. They charge towards us. Star sets off again, leaping as best she can. A few hundred metres further on she takes refuge in an area where blackthorn bushes form a dense thicket with hazels and brambles, an almost impregnable fortress. I can't get in there, but I do see Star. The hounds arrive and, seeing my stance and aggressive posture, they continue on their way without stopping. A moment later, the hunters show up, shouting loudly, accompanied by more dogs on leashes. I leave my rucksack by the entrance to the path along which Star fled. Since it's impregnated with my scent, it will confuse the scent of the pursuing hounds. I hide in a thicket nearby. They pass, my ruse works, and I know they won't be coming back straight away. Out of prudence, we stay hidden for another hour or so, long enough for the beaters to move away for good. I'm extremely worried about my friend. As soon as possible, as evening approaches, I go back to see her. My poor Star ... She's lying a few metres away from me, fatally wounded in the chest. She's trembling, and I still can't get into her hiding place. I talk to her, reminding her of the good times we have had together.

'Thanks, my little Star, for everything you brought me, your knowledge, your friendship, you respect, your love.'

' . . . '

I try to make my voice sound reassuring but I'm suffering in the depths of my soul. I know that in that part of her body the wound is too serious for me to attempt an intervention. She looks at me affectionately and then raises her head slightly. A few rays of sunlight struggle to cross the sky and the scents in the upper air don't reach her nostrils. A few birds fly through the soft air. My eyes fill with tears. And I'm filled with a form

death of a deer by hunter. He soothes her with his words.

of hatred, because I'm aware that she will never know all the pleasures, all the joys that I had imagined for her. The life gradually slips from her body. She looks at me, uttering little sobbing cries, before resting her head on the ground. Star struggles to breathe amid the vibrating waves of evening. She starts to fall asleep in the still, grey day. My friend lies on the damp, frozen ground of autumn.

'Oh, forgive me, Star, I wasn't able to protect you. I wasn't strong enough. Forgive me.'

' . . . '

'I promise I'll look after Chévi. He's only five months old. I'll take care of him so that he grows up, gets big and strong and has his own territory. A fine territory. I promise you, my friend. I promise.'

Her sadness is there, perceptible in the things around her. The grass doesn't stir, no new light plays in the thickening mist, no particular scent imbues the cold air, and yet a great weariness lies upon the forest. She is tired, she is in pain, all around her desolation spreads like a toxic miasma. The clouds are still forming low in the sky, reddish against the pale November air. My friend closes her eyes . . . The sun has just set. My Star has gone out, but she will shine for ever in my heart and, I hope, up there in the sky of the Great Island. She lived her life fighting the dog days of summer, the darkness of the long winter nights and all the events that she confronted with the same strength and the same courage. Let those who walk in the forest, and whose eyes have met those of a deer, think for a moment about her life, shattered by a bullet on an

THE killing of a gentle animal -

autumn day that had begun so well. Life in the wild is like that, and in this natural world that I love so much, at once so lovely and so cruel and to which the woods bear witness, I say to myself that if the trees could weep, rivers of tears would flow in our forests.

I stay there, by my friend's lifeless corpse, for several long minutes. I have to move poor Star out of her thicket. I know the hunters will come in search of her. They know they hit her; they will go looking for her with bloodhounds and follow her trail until they find her corpse. I take my friend in my arms to bury her far from the site of the hunt, in a place where no one is likely to find her. The twenty kilos I am carrying are too heavy for me, and it's exhausting. My strength is failing me, but I don't want my friend to end up in a freezer and then on someone's plate. She deserves better than that. Her name was Star. I hold her tightly and redouble my efforts. Once I've reached my destination, I break the ground with the survival knife that I carry with me at all times, and then continue digging by hand, but the ground is too hard. I can't break through the layer of clay and flint to make a deep enough hole. I set Star in the shallow trench I've made and then camouflage her body with two palisades of fir-tree branches bound together with linen twine, then bring them together to make a kind of little roof, a discreet grave. I cover the whole thing over with soil, moss and bracken, hoping that the rotting smell of the body doesn't attract a stray dog over the next few days.

It's raining, I'm drenched, I'm shivering, but I want to join Six-Points, Daguet and poor Chévi, now motherless. I search all night, and find them at last in the early morning. They fled, too, when the hunt began, and I'm happy to find them alive. They're there, safe and sound. Daguet and Chévi are lying down. Six-Points, standing upright, lifts his head. I don't know if he can smell my emotion or the scent of Star's blood on my clothes, but he comes towards me, frightened and trembling, sniffs me for a few seconds and runs off barking. I am overcome and I weep. I'm afraid I've lost a friend. Maybe he'll think I killed his companion? He will have gone in search of her, but I know he will never find her, because Star is no more. Daguet and Chévi don't seem troubled by my presence, nor even by the pestilential smell that I must certainly be giving off by now. With this ceaseless rain the blood on my clothes won't dry, and the rucksack containing my change of clothes is buried more than a kilometre away. I'd like to go there, but I can't leave Daguet and Chévi on their own. Common sense demands that I should go and look for that rucksack, but I can't bring myself to leave.

A few hours later, Six-Points is back. He comes over to me, looks at me for a long time, sniffs my clothes as he walks around me and then licks my bloodied trousers. It's then that I realise that he's understood. I don't know how, but his entire attitude shows me that he knows now. Then my sadness mingles with a feeling of joy. He isn't angry with me, and our friendship hasn't been affected. We spend the morning together with the sorrow and gloom that I'm sure I must be involuntarily communicating to the group, then I make up my mind to go and find my bag anyway. It's stupid to keep dirty clothes on, and in any case it won't change anything. I wash my clothes with the rain that's still falling a little. I put on clean, dry clothes, then light a little fire to heat up a tin and, more importantly, to dry my old clothes.

I didn't imagine that the time would come when I would take such pleasure in eating food from a heated tin. When you haven't had any food for a long time and the hunger becomes too insistent, your response to taste sensations is surprising. All flavours are heightened. Salt, sugar, pepper – all those tastes explode in your mouth like a firework. Six-Points and Chévi join me. Near the still-smoking embers is a charred log, and they hurry to eat it. It's a far from negligible source of carbon, so scarce in nature that they seem just as satisfied as I am. Six-Points greedily lowers his head over the tin, but there's nothing left in it but some sauce for him to lick.

The three of us spend the rest of the afternoon together. Six-Points seems still to be looking for his companion, and Chévi utters little squeaking sobs that make my heart ache every time. I don't know how, but Six-Points manages to find Star's trail. He takes the same route as we did the previous day when the hunt arrived, then recovers his tracks and finds the grave that I built for Star. He paces around it with Chévi, who recognises his mother's scent. He makes little whispering sounds, no doubt hoping that his mother will reply. I'm sorry to see that, and overwhelmed. I'm filled with guilt: I wasn't able to protect her. After a few hours we set off again without looking back. I have a feeling that a page of our story has been turned, and I can't accept it. The days follow on from one another, Six-Points and his life force teach me that you need to move on. You have to remember the best of people that you have known without ever missing them. There are so many daily deaths in nature that you would spend your whole time weeping if you stopped each time someone was lost. Life goes on. Now Six-Points will take Chévi under his wing. The little one will spend winter and spring with his father, even more of a presence in his life than he had been before that cursed day.

The companion to star with sadness teaches him that you need to move on.

You have to remember the best of people that you have known without ever missing them

Life goes on

our economic development
contemporary demographics
hunting / forestry
have deeply altered the
behavior of the deer + cause
them to live in a landscape

12

of fear
Risk of being seen
danger of roads
lack of food
" of shelter
} have hidden
their
enjoyment
of life

After the terrible trauma of the loss of my friend Star, I can't accept the idea that this is what life is like. In spite of a long meditation on my vision of life, the reality of the landscape forces me to accept the loss of the creatures dearest in my eyes, and my heart is hardened by harmful emotions. How can I accept the death of my friends without doing anything about it? Anger rumbles in the depths of my soul. My friends and I regularly experience shooting parties during the winter season, and I realise that I have the same feelings and the same fears as my companions. Since mid-November I've been living in a kind of perpetual fear that a van might appear on a forest path. A forestry barrier creaking and breaking the morning silence at some unexpected hour immediately awakens my instinct for survival. People shouting or dogs barking in the distance immediately make me think of that sword of Damocles. Every day from autumn onwards I pray that we won't be caught up in tragedy again. However much

I might try and remind myself that fear doesn't avoid danger, my feelings are still too powerful, and I can't yet rid myself of the burden that weighs on me until the start of spring, the end of the hunting season. Living in the heart of the lives of the roe deer, I notice that in spite of apparent 'controlled cynegetic management', in the new-fangled hunting jargon, my friends are still misunderstood and very much disdained. Listed like trees (above twenty per hundred hectares they have to be culled), then hunted on the grounds of space regulation and trapped in the forest behind fences along the forest's edge to limit the possible 'destruction' that they might cause to cultivated fields, they have now become an 'accident-creating factor' along the countless roads that run through their territories. Seeing them in these terms – as we would wish to see them, rather than as they are – is too simplistic, too unrealistic and, let's admit it, inhumane. Whether they live by the sea, in the mountains, in valleys or on vast open plains, roe deer conquer different micro-habitats such as bushes, gardens, orchards and fields, not thanks to the constraints of our civilisation but because of them.

The roe deer is an extremely intelligent animal with exceptional, unique qualities, and it adapts to everything, or almost everything. The proof is that it has developed the ability to live near humans where other wild animals faced with similar conditions have declined and sometimes even disappeared. The uniqueness of its social life, which is both individualistic and gregarious, the talents that it develops in order to take advantage of its environment and optimise its territory, the nature of its population, which it develops according to temporal or spatial changes to its habitat thanks to a mode of reproduction unique among cervids – all of these features make roe deer unusually ecologically adaptable. However, our desire to control populations, along with galloping urbanisation, put these animals in a state of constant fear. The risk of being seen, the danger of roads, food shortages, lack of shelter and, of course, death. This anxiety-inducing environment leads them to make compromises between all these dangers and ways in which they might otherwise benefit. Our economic development, contemporary demographics, hunting and forestry deeply alter the behaviour of my friends and cause them to live in a landscape of fear.

After several shooting parties we go elsewhere for a few days to seek refuge, and don't return to our home range until the dead of night. Roe deer become anxious, fearful and stressed during the hunting season. The most experienced of them, such as Daguet or Six-Points, start observing the behaviour of humans along the forest paths to see whether or not there is any danger. In fact, the regularity of the appearance of runners or hikers can become an indicator of danger. They stop coming into the forest on hunting days. So their absence becomes a reliable indication of the presence of hunters. To an extent, present-day hunts artificialise the behaviour of roe deer. My friends move less during the winter season; they learn by heart every square metre of their territory and make refuges for themselves in well-situated thickets, so that they can hide there in the event of a shoot. Wild populations can't be controlled, because 'the only way we can command nature is by obeying it'. And to do that we have to see the roe deer as they are and make these marvellous animals responsible for their own management.

When you live like a roe deer, the hunt feels a bit like a tornado. You don't know where it's going to go or how much damage it's going to cause, and there is nothing you can do to prevent it in advance. For all those reasons I decided to teach my friends some tricks to recognise and avoid the beaters before they began. To start these lessons, I choose Six-Points, an intelligent and experienced deer, with whom I've shared some dramatic events, including the loss of his companion, Star.

In the life of a deer, there are days when you're the leader. In the winter, groups form, without the appointment of a leader as such. Nonetheless, a management committee is established according to the character of each individual. By a form of consensus, an individual then becomes 'the boss'. A point of reference in a way, who has the necessary knowledge and experience. And that knowledge is beyond dispute, because it will be placed at the service of all the deer in the group. The deer that inherits this responsibility is generally the most experienced at protecting the group, and the most likely to fill their stomachs, because he knows the best feeding areas.

The deer that constitute a group are deeply autonomous and very dependent on each other, and each one fills their role individually. Life becomes more instinctive and has a direct connection with nature. Information is exchanged between one deer and another, but the main preoccupation is to stay alive and maintain one's own equilibrium. There are no inferiors, and no slaves. Each deer is a complete individual, one who makes choices, and the sum total of those individual choices ensures the cohesion of the group.

While I'm sharing a moment with Six-Points, Arrow and Velvet, a young buck with whom I'm just becoming acquainted, four vans driving at low speed pass in front of us, along a logging path. At this hour of the morning it can't be a simple woodcutting operation. A hunt is underway. It

Chévi and Fern on the path towards la Crutte. Crossing a path is always a delicate matter. You mustn't be seen or scented by a predator. Sound and smell help us to sense the general atmosphere of a forest. But take care: a calm forest isn't a forest that's free from danger.

appears that today I'm the leader, and that's fine with me. My three companions are resting and ruminating in the undergrowth. Then I decide to take everyone to the patch of pines so that every whisper I make is heeded, and the smell of my body is not too diluted by the wind. I know from experience that deer are sensitive to our moods, and more particularly to the *scent* of our moods. In fact, when we are aggressive or stressed, the scent of our bodies is rather acidic, like that of an onion, while a happy or peaceful mood will give off sweet, subtle aromas like those of a gourmet patisserie. Posture also plays a large part. If I turn in a circle, scratching the ground while panting and looking at the horizon on all sides, that conveys unease more clearly than if I sit down cross-legged and yawn or pluck leaves. The fawns learn to detect all of that with their mother or their elders from a very young age. All I have to do is make sure they understand what I have to say to them.

I don't have much time before the beaters begin. I notice that the hunters have left their vehicles and their weapons unsupervised by the spot at the top of a hill where hunts used to meet when they were carried out on horseback. While the men take up posts at regular intervals along the paths for the shoot, I lead Six-Points near one of the vans so that he can sniff the smells of the powder and the death of other animals that have fallen in previous hunts. Along the way I lose Velvet and Arrow who, I understand, are very frightened. I make Six-Points smell the scent of a Teflon-lined jacket hanging on the wing mirror of a 4×4 and try to communicate my anxiety and my fear. The scent of my stress-induced perspiration is enough to convey the sense of danger. I want to make him associate this smell with hunting. Then we pass by an elevated stand of trees which I climb up and down several times, uttering regular little cries, as the young deer do to call their mothers when they are worried. I want him to grasp the fact that a human might be above his head, and that it's worrying. In fact, deer don't always think of looking into the air when walking; scents don't come down all the way to their nostrils and they can be shot without even being aware that they're being hunted. I return to the pine grove about twenty metres along the path that we're now walking along. Through the faded bracken I show him the men posted on the edge of the forest, sitting on their little folding stools with their rifles. Six-Points is pressing against me and I feel his heart beating very hard against my shoulder. He looks at me and sniffs me, and looks uneasily at this strange procedure going on before our very eyes. The hairs on his rump are erect, which tells me that he's aware of the danger.

A quarter of an hour later, the beaters start, and we are still standing in front of the marksmen. Since the vegetation is very tall, we have the advantage of seeing without being seen. A boar scurries about thirty metres to our right. He's going down into a little valley. A first shot rings out, then a second. I bark faintly, imitating the danger signal. We set off quickly through the brambles to get up the hill to safety. The shouts of the hunters make our heart race a bit more. Six-Points starts moving away from me; he wants to flee.

Then I bark twice in his direction, which in roe deer language means: stay in a group. He stops quickly and decides to trust me. At last I can reveal the key to my hunt-sab plan. I run off to an area of the forest which, in theory at least, the hunters are not allowed to enter. He follows me and it fills me with joy. There's nothing to fear here, and I show by my scent that I feel much better, that I feel at ease. I sit down and relax. We stay in safety for a moment and wait for it to pass. I'm surprised by the trust that Six-Points places in me. He has barely listened to his own instincts, and has decided to put his faith in everything that I've suggested. I'm lucky to have a friend like him. A few hours later, we hear the hunters moving off in the distance. The hunting horns sound the end of the chase and we spend a calm afternoon. At nightfall, my day as leader comes to an end. Six-Points will find his family. We look for the 'survivors', hoping that my friends are still alive. Today two roe deer were killed, along with eight boar and five red stags. That fills me with deep sadness. I hope that Six-Points has understood my message, and that next time he will reproduce the survival plan that I taught him.

A few weeks later, when the beaters take us by surprise, I realise with joy that Six-Points understood very clearly. He understood the vans, he sensed the dangerous atmosphere of the barking dogs, the smell of gunpowder and all those elements that make a day so sad. To my great surprise, I notice that he's leading Chévi, Arrow, Daguet and others into the hunting-free zone that I showed him. I know that Six-Points is an intelligent and audacious deer, but I never imagined that he would have the ability to pass his knowledge on to the other deer. Today, the hunters failed to hit a single roe deer, and I'm proud of the fact.

13

This particular winter I only left my forest three times. First because there was no longer anything to be gained from my visits to civilisation. Walking five kilometres for a bowl of fromage blanc with a handful of muesli makes no sense. When you're trying to optimise your chances of survival, you can't afford the luxury of wasting energy, even if the idea of spending a few hours in the warm is always seductive. Besides, I no longer need to stock up on food as frequently as I did at the start of my adventure. I know how to manage my stores of dead wood and dried fruits, and I'm no longer worried about shortages. Now, since the first cold spells, my metabolism has slowed down to adapt to these three months of scarcity. I move less, I eat less, and my stores of processed food have become almost useless. Finally, under the ceaseless assault of the cold and damp, my rechargeable batteries have given up the ghost, pouring their toxic contents into the camera. So I've drawn a line under my activity as a photographer. There is a single reason why I still go back and forth between the forest and the world of human beings: to stock up on matches. You can't spend the winter without fire, you would risk dying of cold.

Luckily spring has arrived. Nature wakes up and all the living creatures in the forest are filled with a kind of joy. With the first rising sap, the first opening bud, an invisible presence enters us. Everyone is happy to come back to life. The birds sing differently, the sounds of the forest are more open. Different species come together. It's as if the whole of nature is saying 'hello' to itself. I go for a walk in the middle of the forest where Daguet usually sleeps. Along the way I collect sap from several silver birches. I used a gimlet to dig a little hole a centimetre deep about twenty centimetres from the ground. In that I placed a little straw that allows the sap to flow into a water bottle tied just below it. If the tree is big and generous I can get a good litre in a single night. The juice is deliciously sweet for someone who has lost the habit of consuming the enormous quantities of sugar that you find in supermarket food. This drink gives me all the essential minerals that I have so cruelly lacked during the winter. A litre of this juice gives me an incredible boost for the day. I also like to lick the sap that runs down the trunks of the pine trees. It provides a bit more sugar, and mixed with the silver-birch sap I find it has an astonishing flavour, with a springlike freshness. Having said that, you've got to work quickly because as soon as the first leaves appear at the top of the tree the sap stops flowing.

I continue on my morning round, and at last I come across Daguet, who is clearly very embarrassed, because Chévi, now one year old, is marking his first territory, and doesn't seem to have understood the rules of the game. For a few weeks Fern, Daguet's little sister, who was born shortly after Chévi, goes for a walk on Daguet's territory, which is just an annex to their mother's. That means that Fern is protected by her big brother. Except that Chévi has plainly fallen in love with the young damsel and is invading poor Daguet's territory. He's already been thrown out several times, but Chévi is so besotted that he keeps coming back. And sometimes it's even Fern who draws him into her home range, which is Daguet's territory. It all seems very complicated, and Chévi and Fern's emotional future seems to be compromised. That's without taking Daguet's big heart into account, however: seeing that there is no point in keeping Chévi outside his territory, he finally lets him woo his sister while also protecting him against potential competitors.

I am contemplating this scene from daily life when all of a sudden Chévi, intrigued by my presence, approaches slowly, sniffs me and walks around me in a circle. I turn on my axis to go on observing him without craning my neck. For some time he has agreed to let me walk behind him, but only at a distance of about twenty metres. It occurs to me that the time may have come to take things further. Perhaps it's the right day for him. Perhaps he's ready. Three-quarters of an hour has passed and Chévi has started nibbling at the carpet of ferns around me. He stares at me for several minutes at a time with his big black shining eyes. Roe deer don't use their eyesight as much as their cousins the red deer to notice movement, but his slightly protuberant eyes as well as his long, flexible neck give him an excellent panoramic view of his environment. The structure of his eye consists almost entirely of rods, cells that send the brain black and white images, and a few scattered cones which play a part in chromatic vision. That's why Chévi sees shades close to grey more easily than colour itself. It's that anatomical peculiarity that gives him sharper vision at dusk, and allows him to detect movements more quickly.

A pheasant passes elegantly about ten metres away. Chévi, apparently startled, moves away from the bird and comes closer to me. He looks at me for a long time without moving, sniffs the air around him, lowers his head slightly to pick up my scent and understands that the distance between us is really very small. Having said that, he is intelligent and bound to notice that in spite of my proximity I haven't attacked him. Out of caution, he moves a little way away with a very confident gait, a manner of walking that I call the 'firm hoof'. It's a step typical of roe deer which, when they are curious and move closer to something or else further away from it, makes them look proud and, with their slender bodies and their incredibly graceful, slow-motion movements, almost noble; they appear to be stamping the ground. The front hoof rises to the shoulder, then stretches out fully before planting itself confidently on the soil. I take advantage of the moment to get to my feet. He turns again to look at Daguet, shakes his head and presents his antlers to invite him to fight. He seems strong and invincible with his two little antlers which, without tines, look like the horns of a goat. He scrapes the ground with his front hoof in a cloud of dust. Daguet prepares for the game and, just as Chévi lowers his head, barks so loudly at the little buck that he jumps back and runs about twenty metres away before coming back, quivering. I burst out laughing and they both look at me. They're like two kids in a school playground. Chévi is well aware that Daguet is stronger than he is, and that he doesn't need to engage in this kind of jousting. He also knows that the only way to win territory is by cunning, but he enjoys playing so much that he forgets the harsh reality of life as a roe deer. He nonchalantly turns towards Fern, who has been equally jittery. I walk a little way behind them, leaving Daguet to his activities. I move towards Chévi and try to walk less than five metres behind him; he makes a little jump to get away from me. Fern lies down and Chévi goes on marking his territory. The game goes on, then he wants to cross the forest path which, at this time of day, is used by horse riders, cyclists and runners. I follow him. He gives me a sideways look but continues on his way. After a few minutes' reflection, he crosses the path. I run after him. Having reached the other side, he seems intrigued by my stubbornness in following him. He runs a little, climbs the steep path into the recently logged beechwood and hides behind a newly felled pile of wood to eat some accessible leaves. I walk over to eat some leaves opposite him. The unease fades, making way for playfulness. Chévi knows that I live in the forest now, and he can tell the difference between me and all the other humans who visit. Like the other roe deer, he only recognises me, my unique smell, and he runs off immediately if another human tries to approach him. It's as if he's sending me a message: 'I want to find out about you, you can follow me, but be gentle because I'm still a bit fearful.' Message received. I walk less than ten metres behind him.

The sound of the leaves on the ground no longer seems to disturb him, but we're joined by a buck that I don't know very well, a two-year-old. He comes from an area higher up the hill, which I call 'the slopes'. The newcomer observes us from a distance, plainly doesn't want to come any closer and sniffs us a bit, still from a distance. He is muscular and seems suspicious. I'll call him Sus. Chévi observes him while coming closer to me, walks around me at a good distance to hide and also to ensure that I'm between him and Sus. I immediately note Chévi's bravery, but I can't intervene. It's their business. Sus finally comes over to get further acquainted. After a few minutes he tries to chase Chévi off, but my presence gets in the way. In spite of his slightly nervous approach, Sus is determined to chase Chévi, who is still hiding behind me. At last, weary of the fight, Sus gives up and moves away.

I spend the afternoon with Chévi, aware that the encounter with Sus has brought us together, and something tells me that we are about to form a great friendship. I observe him very close up, I study him and take advantage of this magical moment. I place myself upwind of him so that he could more easily sniff my scent, which he seems to like. You have to imagine that Chévi moves in a universe saturated with scents. His slightly wrinkled nostrils, hairless and damp, allow him to

Sus in full flight. His unusual intelligence and his knowledge of the terrain have allowed Sus to escape the hunters and stay alive on more than one occasion.

distinguish all the scents carried on the wind. By definition, damp air carries smells better than dry air. That's why today, in this dry April weather, Chévi constantly licks his nostrils to increase the humidity of his breathing. Sometimes he lifts his muzzle a little to get a clearer definition of the different layers of air. That's how he can tell the behaviour of a human who regularly comes to the forest with an innocent attitude and scent from an individual who enters his territory slyly and furtively. A roe deer downwind of a walker will always know that he is there.

Chévi continues his little territory-marking stroll. Every
now and then he scrapes the ground with his front hoof,
takes a few steps, urinates, rubs his antlers against an eagle
fern and then a young poplar, finishing with an old shrub.
You need to remember that roe deer have a certain number
of scent glands that play an essential part in their daily life.
The gland between the toes of the hoof, the interdigital gland,
secretes a substance that is deposited on the ground. It allows
the members of a family or a group to follow each other, even
when the forest terrain is dense. On the back hoof, level with
the ankle, a small glandular zone concealed by slightly longer
hairs secretes a scent that roe deer leave by brushing against
low vegetation as they move. Every animal, and hence every
human being, is a unique cocktail of scents, an alchemy of
secretions that pass through the pores of the skin when they
sweat. This olfactory print allows the roe deer to locate in
their memory an animal or a human that they have bumped
into before, and therefore recognise. And it is in this way
that I manage to become part of their universe. My clothes,
my equipment, my sweat, my urine are impregnated with
my scent. That scent is mixed with pollen and dust, and the
sap of the plants that I break or crush when walking, which
makes the information the deer receive more complex but
allows them to grasp my position and know which direction
I am travelling in.

After Sus has passed, Chévi leaves his mark with another
glandular area on his forehead. It all asserts his presence. On
ordinary ferns, shrubs and dead branches, Chévi marks his

passage and his territory with this substance which to me smells a bit like apples. It's also what allows bucks like Sus or little females like Fern to show that they have passed along this way. Then he scratches the base of his antlers with his front hoof and presses the hoof down very hard to make a clear print as if to sign his work. The size of these glands increases between May and September, when territorial activity is at its most intense. The rubbing is done against trees whose diameter is no greater than the space between the antlers, and very seldom prevents dense clusters of vegetation forming. Still, if the foresters are mad enough to replant standard deciduous trees on bare ground after a logging operation without putting protection around the plants, well . . . you make your choices!

I stay with him for a few days to learn his territory and the paths he takes. Very gradually, Chévi allows me a degree of complicity which I haven't achieved with the other deer. It's almost as if we'd always known one another. We think about the same things at the same time. Wherever we go we bump into one another without planning to. As if fate were forcing us to get to know each other. One evening, when I've left him with Fern while I'm collecting my little harvest of birch sap, I catch him following me, licking every trunk behind me that has a thin trickle of sap running along the bark. Fern, more fearful but never very far from her lover, is a long way from saying 'hello' to me, but is extremely interested in my activities, and Chévi, as if demonstrating bravado to his Juliet, sets himself challenges such as letting a human walk behind him without being frightened, going so far as to eat from the same blackberry bush as me or approaching my shoes to sniff at them. Personally, I'm not sure that this attitude wins Fern's unconditional approval, but I confess that I'm impressed by the behaviour, because no individual roe deer has ever shown such interest in me or been so quick to let me approach it.

In a few weeks we move from a state of fear to a progressive trust before ending up with complete and total friendship. Now Chévi makes me a part of his life. I can play with him, walking beside him, eat blackberries side by side with him and all kinds of other things. Sometimes I even feel that there are fewer barriers between Chévi and me than there are between Chévi and Fern. He makes me feel a bit like a roe deer. Fully integrated. I'm quite at ease with him. He doesn't judge me, and even gives me the impression that he understands me. We are blood brothers. An inseparable trio forms and we spend an incredible April, full of joy, friendship and mutual discoveries.

Chevi the deer he can
play with
walk beside
eat with
Strong friendship &
complete trust
can sense thru my
scent & posture when
there is danger

14

Ever stronger bonds of friendship form between me and Chévi, and our curiosity about one another brings us closer every day. Chévi observes me and learns from me at incredible speed. He accepts all my movements and my scents, to the point where we can communicate more easily with one another. I learn little whispers or grunts that I didn't hear with Daguet or Six-Points. And one remarkable thing: he listens to me sing and talk to him. He even seems to associate my words with my actions. When we cross a forest path and I say to him, 'Right, careful, because there are humans,' he associates my unease, my scent and my general posture with the situation of the moment and the imminence of danger, even though he hasn't understood the actual words that I've said. When I crouch down behind him and say quietly, 'All right, Chévi?' he stops, looks at me tenderly with his little head on one side, licking his muzzle. His eyes sparkle and he seems to be replying, 'Sure, fine! And you?' I realise the extent to which roe deer communicate with one another. Paying attention, I note that they communicate more by sound than sight, because they can be very noisy about it. They yelp to ask questions, to challenge one another to a game or simply out of curiosity. A series of barks accompanied by marked little jumps indicates danger to all the other bucks and does in the vicinity. Fawns with their mothers make little whispering noises so as not to get lost when they move around or when they get bored. If they're frightened, they utter a louder little cry, a kind of sharp and rhythmic squawk, not unlike the cry of the tree creeper. The purpose of those sounds is to make their mother come running even though it might be dangerous. During the rutting season, in July/August, a buck's breathing develops a very striking whistle. He grunts and sometimes groans to himself. A doe on heat makes different cries, little whistling sounds, slightly hoarse and plaintive. Pursued by a rutting male she utters a more ringing yelp, a little cry from the heart that is difficult to describe.

Chévi allows me to understand the mentality of roe deer, and I very soon learn to imitate their language. Those complex codes with precise intervals of sound are not easy to pick up. I never call a roe deer friend in the same way every day, because you have to take into consideration the influence of climate, temperature, wind, weather and, even more difficult to sense, atmospheric pressure. To this we might add honesty towards roe deer. It's not about barking stupidly and selfishly to attract your friends, but about knowing what you want to say, do or make them understand when they reply.

He learns to imitate the
sounds of the roe deer

Chévi at night. Night-time arouses the senses. The senses of smell and hearing, but also of touch, particularly the feel of the plants that I need to recognise by moonlight.

They don't always appreciate false alarms and I don't want to let them down. At the same time, it's hard to find grumpy roe deer, because happiness seems to be their natural state. Nor is it a matter of giving orders to Chévi, because I don't want to reduce him to the rank of a domestic animal. He wouldn't obey me in any case, he's as stubborn as a billy goat. In this story I am, after all, the companion animal, and I'm the one walking behind the wild animals, not the other way around. Sometimes I confess that it would suit me very well if they listened to me, because roe deer are so adventurous when they strike out for new territories that they sometimes throw caution to the wind. They're not oblivious, but they're reckless. For his own safety I've already tried to dissuade Chévi from going to places that are too dangerous, like sports grounds, the edges of roads or tracks across the clearing in the middle of the afternoon. Even by blocking his path, there's nothing to be done and then I ask myself: who am I to stop him doing anything? We will agree together that the best thing about freedom and life in the wild is never to be given constraints or orders even if there is danger everywhere. Living is dangerous in itself, so why keep him from living? There are already plenty of obstacles in nature.

Talking of natural barriers, there's one that Chévi hadn't for a second imagined, and that's Sus. He seems to have set his cap at Fern, who doesn't seem to be rejecting the handsome fellow's advances. Chévi and Sus are very different characters. One is affectionate, a little childish, slim and cunning, and

tried to dissuade Chévi from
going to places too dangerous
by blocking his path

very tender. The other is more brutal, mature and macho, hefty and direct. Sus has also established his territory directly beside the one belonging to Daguet who, let me remind you, protects Chévi. It risks being a long and complicated story for my friends. Fern, since she's the one in this story who has to decide which of the two suitors is most deserving of her, has chosen to alternate between them. One day Chévi, one day Sus and, what's more, the two Don Juans agree on one point: the situation is not sustainable. This late spring coexistence is tense, and Fern finally decides to isolate herself for the summer. At the same time Sus abandons his territory. It's too risky to live alongside Daguet, who can be very discouraging, and even more so with a barking, groaning neighbour like Six-Points. Chévi is opportunistically taking over Sus's territory, which is now vacant, and seems already to have found his feet. I find him surprisingly intelligent and cunning. Here he is, the owner of twenty hectares of territory for which he hasn't had to fight once. Half of it is protected by Daguet, and the other has been left unoccupied by its former owner. Worth taking risks from time to time.

A few days later Chévi surprises me again. I'm walking behind him and Fern in a patch of beech trees. They're eating a few leaves here and there, particularly wood anemones. This plant, a member of the ranunculus family, is consumed in large quantities by my friends because it contains a tannin that lets the roe deer purge themselves of enteritis, an illness not unlike our own gastroenteritis, but generally fatal to roe deer. The plant grows in the gloom of damp undergrowth, and not all roe deer have access to it because of the nature of their territories, particularly the ones that live in coniferous forests with acid soil. Chévi and Fern, their stomachs full, look for a calm, serene place where they can chew the cud in peace. Fern lies down against a little pile of recently cut logs. Chévi looks around him, but nowhere seems suitable. He ventures over to a little slope, and I follow him, simplest thing in the world. Having arrived a few metres behind him, I crouch down. It's then that he decides to turn around to come and see me. He stops just in front of me, studies me and sniffs. He grooms himself a little and looks furtively around. After a few minutes he takes a step forward, shivers slightly and looks at me. I don't recognise this posture and haven't seen it in any other roe deer. He lifts his head and then lowers it to the ground to sniff the different scents he finds there. He steps forward gently, walks around me and goes on sniffing at me, his unease overcome by his curiosity. He comes over to my face and starts licking it. I can feel his hot, sweet little tongue passionately caressing my skin. I can feel his hot and rhythmical breathing, while my heart is beating at a rate of knots. It's the first time a roe deer has shown me such affection. A great happiness, a joy, fullness, pride, no words can describe what I feel at that moment. Thousands of emotions run trembling down my spine. With these little strokes of his tongue Chévi is washing and 'tasting' me so that he can remember my unique scent, which will seal our friendship for ever. His tongue passes over my eyes, my ears, my nose, and then he examines my lips. He very delicately removes my hat, sniffs my hair, plays with it a little and runs his head under the collar of my jumper to reach my neck. Then it's over and the grooming is complete. A few moments later, while I stroke his chest, Chévi looks at me, clearly satisfied with this exchange, then lies down right at my feet. Still crouching, I sit cross-legged to ensure that my legs don't go numb. Something unique is happening between us, and from his sparkling eyes I know that our relationship is one of trust, respect and goodwill, key assets in a successful friendship between a roe deer and a human being.

Deer licking his face (Chévi)
showing affection
I stroke him friendship
Our relationship has been
sealed. Trust / respect /
Goodwill has been
exchange between a
roe deer + a human being

He lies down with the deer + abandon (they) themselves entirely in nature

Huge pleasure He gets from living with the Roe deer especially one deer who has taught him about his weaknesses/strengths desires

15

One fine afternoon in early summer, Chévi and I are walking in a grove under the light, spreading branches of a magnificent birch. Chévi lies down at the end of the trunk of a big tree felled by the last winter storm. We look at each other for a moment. I really wonder what might have led him to want to tame me more than any other roe deer before him. Does he sense the huge pleasure I get from living with him, dragged into this unusual adventure which is teaching me a bit more about myself every day, changing the perception I might have of my weaknesses, my strengths and even my desires? Does he share my wish to want to learn more about him? The treetops dance slightly in a warm south wind, and a shadow with a hint of green passes over his face and vanishes again. I lie down on the ground, with my back on a bed of ferns, and contemplate the translucent tangle of emerald foliage. We stay there for a long time, lying under the sun-dappled trees, taking advantage of this magical, enchanted moment to abandon ourselves

The joy + peace he feels
by his next to his companion
Deer

entirely to nature, and letting the weight of the constraints of life in the wild slip from us. Absolutely nothing can describe that joy or the peace that enters me then. We spend the afternoon enjoying the time passing gently until sunset.

We get up, still drowsy from our luxurious repose, a little dazed by the calm that has settled around us. We walk together through the thicket in the wood. I push aside the ferns that are absorbing the freshness of the evening, and allow myself to be filled by the warm smells that have accumulated during the day. Now cool, now lukewarm and humid, the air impregnated with the honeyed aroma of the grasses, both coarse and tender, makes my head spin. At this time of day when you're never really sure if it's day or night, the blue tits, the robins, the chaffinches and all the other birds gradually fall silent to make way for the deep silence of night. All the sounds fade into the scented cool of the shadow that falls around me. The entire forest has woken up, yet not a sound disturbs this serenity. We walk and make our way into different layers of the forest as night continues to fall. Nightjars flit nervously over the clearing that we're passing through, leaving their daytime retreat to go in search of insects, breaking the monotony with their very particular call, like the purring of a cat.

A few moments later we pause in the middle of the oak wood where a male tawny owl is hooting loudly. A female joins in with these calls in a duet that makes the darkness ring, and another couple respond in the distance. Once it's pitch dark, these formidable hunters become the terror of little rodents. Later, an owl, its wings beating silently, creates a faint

The trees / the Roots / the Trunks
he feels he's become one with nature
at me

draught above my head. The full moon casts its pale light on the undergrowth, my shadow appearing on it like a ghost. The forest's aspect shifts, its features alter. My own senses are on alert tonight, each step carrying me further into a cathedral of trees. I feel the roots moving under my feet. I hear the trunks creak like rigging when a zephyr stirs the canopy. The trees are communicating with one another. Am I the subject of their conversation? Everything encourages reveries in this magical and mysterious universe.

Chévi brings me back to reality when, with a series of little whispers, he lets me know that we need to get a move on if we're to get to wherever he wants to go. If I don't respond,

Two neighbours. Fouilliou and Mimine are badgers that I encountered regularly. For them, I was one of the forest dwellers, and did not represent a threat.

Badgers / Rodents / Small mammals
Owls / Insects / boar
Birds / Fox

It's a magical + mysterious universe
contemplate the stars

he comes over, lowers his head, stretches his neck as if to sniff my shoes and snorts before setting off again at a trot for several metres. During a brief pause, I doze nearby, and while I'm sleeping a shrew, the world's smallest mammal, slips into my trouser leg to take advantage of my body warmth for a while. I seem to be running a guest house for small mammals. There are two ways of being woken up in that situation: with a squeak and a swift getaway, or sometimes with a grateful little bite.

Moments later we climb a little path that leads to a thinly wooded platform. From up there, under a crystal sky, I contemplate the stars. The tops of the fir trees that line the glade form a pretty dark brown frame that makes the starry sky seem even brighter. Chévi looks at me and raises his head slightly, just as a shooting star passes overhead. I make a wish – I hope it will come true – that we can be friends for life and nothing will ever part us. I will look after you and protect you with all my might, I know that we will have our best times together, and that nothing and no one will ever take them away from us.

Dawn approaches, and the faintly orange light of dawn sharpens the outlines of the forest, still cool and damp. We reach the exposed clay slopes to take advantage of the first rays of the sun, which is shyly appearing over the neighbouring hill. The mists of the Seine and the Eure mingle and evaporate as the sun's first rays settle on the surface of the lakes and ponds below. In the distance I hear roosters crowing to announce the start of a fine day, while the village church at

Friends for life

the bottom of the valley rings out its first chime. A black fox returns from what seems to have been a good night's hunting. The last boar cross the meadows and the dew-drenched fields to reach the depths of the forest before humanity awakens. In the summer the days are long ...

I am no longer welcomed at home

16

The atmosphere at home has suddenly become terribly oppressive. I'm clearly no longer welcome. So to avoid getting in anyone's way I only go there if absolutely necessary, always at night, and I'm as quick as possible. A quick wash, a bowl of fromage blanc wolfed down in seconds, I nick some matches if I find any and go without leaving a trace. Everything in the house makes me nervous. The smells assault my senses now, the clicking of the various electrical devices irritates me, I'm even bothered by the light. I don't think I can bear the world of humans any more. I feel so much better in the woods.

Thanks to Daguet, Six-Points, Chévi and all the others, I can sleep outside now, without a sleeping bag, without a shelter and without heating. They have taught me to live, eat and sleep in brief cycles, which makes life – or survival – possible without too much physical hardship. It's impossible to build a shack or make a fire each time you stop, only to abandon

they have taught him to live/eat/sleep in brief cycles

it after a few hours, and the idea of setting up a base camp is pointless. That doesn't stop me making a palisade with some bits of wood and string to shield myself against the wind, or building a little makeshift shelter in case of a big storm. But it does take time and energy. If I do engage in that kind of work, it's only because I'm soaked, because I want to dry the various layers of my clothing, and because the temperature has become unbearable. Leaving aside the fact that at this stage of my adventure nobody, absolutely nobody, is concerned with my life in this forest, I'm now afraid of attracting the attention of human beings, and it would be unwise to leave evidence that I've passed through. My routes within the undergrowth follow the paths of boar and deer, where I can hide easily. I'm as cautious and pernickety as the roe deer when it comes to crossing a forest path by day, because my worst nightmare would be to be spotted by the forest ranger, even if he doesn't appear on the terrain very often. So I opt for this motto: 'To live happily, live hidden!'

Surviving outside isn't an impossible task. The essential thing is to have good equipment and be organised. You need to know how to save your energy, control your heartbeat with slow breathing, adapt your pace in the coldest days of winter, because perspiration becomes your worst enemy. I don't have the option of migrating to the sun in autumn like the geese do, their flight forming a V for 'voyage', inviting us to dream of far-off lands. I can't live in slow motion like some animals such as dormice, marmots or hedgehogs, which are lucky enough to be able to sleep while winter and its storms rage outside. I

He stays hidden because he is fearful he will be spotted

Fern in the mist. Mist is a valuable ally. Scents travel through the air thanks to the micro-droplets contained in the high levels of humidity. It means that roe deer can sense human presence even before they can see it.

Winter challenges: Stay ing warm/finding enough to eat.

have to get by on my own with what I have to hand and wait for it to pass, with two major challenges: staying warm and finding enough to eat. Sleeping for a long time both by day and by night is potentially lethal, particularly in winter. Lying down, your cardiac rhythm diminishes and, within half an hour, you will feel the effects of the cold. In a few hours, your feet and hands grow cold and numb and then, progressively, you're in a state of hypothermia. Isolating yourself from the ground is therefore of huge importance, so like the roe deer I scrape the ground with my foot to get rid of the layer of fallen vegetation. The earth itself is a warmer and less damp carpet than rotting leaves. I lay down some branches from a fir or another coniferous tree that allow you to isolate yourself from the ground and return your bodily warmth. Thanks to my jumpers I'm able to sleep for several hours despite the temperature, but when it gets really cold the hours of sleep are very short, and sleeping has to be done by day. I take advantage of the late morning rays of sunlight, the warmest ones, to sleep a little. I often wake up feeling groggy and a bit numb, but still happy to have taken advantage of that moment of peace. Sometimes I don't sleep at all. I just snooze for a few minutes, sitting cross-legged under a few bundles of twigs to protect myself against the wind, and then I set off again.

Where food is concerned it's exactly the same principle because I can't fabricate a food store. So moving when the roe deer move becomes a habit. Because of the intensity of the seasons, if the autumn and winter don't provide enough food, I'm forced to move with them, which is entirely incompatible

sleeping long is lethal (hypotherm in winter

roam with the Deer
a nomad

with the idea of a base camp. But that doesn't bother me at all. I find it easier to adapt to the terrain and become a nomad. When the winter is drawn out and food supplies are scarce, the deer are forced to go and feed from cultivated fields. They might be winter crops like rape or root vegetables, or equally weeds. But once the shoots have reached a height of about ten centimetres, the roe deer move on to something else. In the spring the plants will grow, and the trauma dealt them will disappear in a few weeks. Except that since winter is the time when farmers spray their fields with crop protection chemicals, the deer only adopt that strategy as a last resort. For older bucks like Six-Points, Velvet or Valloux, the older forests with their fruit trees, oaks or chestnuts are a godsend, and I come to terms with all that because, when the spring vegetation grows back and abundant food returns, they set off back to the woods to defend last year's territory. As for the does, they can remain for several more weeks in the fields where they found refuge with their fawns, and, if they feel safe, if they aren't troubled too often by passing humans, they can even spend the whole summer there. So a doe without a partner can leave in search of a buck that already has a territory to persuade him to follow her and bring him to the mating zone of her choice. We should remember that roe deer have every little effect on agricultural yields (less than 5 per cent). On the other hand, farm machinery causes terrible damage to roe deer, particularly to the fawns, which can be accidentally crushed. Fields of alfalfa or meadow grass are particularly attractive to young deer, because they establish their resting areas there, and fatalities from machines can nearly halve the annual growth of a population.

Roe deer are very attached to their territory and display great intelligence when it comes to not being noticed. They have an incredible memory, and it's greater when they are on their own terrain. With a strong kinaesthetic sense (an awareness of their own body and its relationship to their surroundings), they know their environment off by heart. They can run and leap at a hundred kilometres an hour along their usual paths without looking at obstacles on the ground or even needing to think about them. This muscle memory that we know to a lesser extent, because it's how we can find the light switch at night or avoid bumping into the foot of the bed, is an enormous help to roe deer, particularly when they are pursued by a predator. Besides, since he has no mirror in which to admire his antlers, the buck must remember their position, their shape and their length, because once they have been stripped of the velvet that covers them they lose all tactile sensitivity.

I also observe that Chévi and many other roe deer are also capable of memorising the best feeding places, as well as the position of the trees that give them the best quantities of foliage and fruits. This behaviour tends to demonstrate that they remember experiences that they have had in the course of previous seasons, sometimes over a period of more than six years, according to the variety of timber species and explains certain psychological disturbances in the case of regular logging on their territory. The change of timetable (summer and winter time) can disturb them for a few days, or even a few weeks. At the time of their greatest activity, as we all know, they lead a crepuscular life; if they regularly cross a road at 7.30 a.m. and the traffic is light at that time, when the clocks change it will be 8.30 and the traffic will be heavier. This is a potentially fatal time for roe deer even if some, more observant than others, very quickly change their schedules so as not to be beside the road when the traffic is bad. Unfortunately, this isn't true of all wild animals, and too many die on the roads.

Deer great intelligence when it comes to not being noticed
② incredible memory
③ strong kinaesthetic sense (awareness of their own body & its relationship to their surroundings)
④ remember experiences that they have had in the past (ex. best place to find food)

17

It's spring, a light wind from the south-west, warm and humid, carries to me the delicate perfume of wood anemones, pilewort and other flowers of the undergrowth. I let the warm rays of sunlight stroke my face as if to convince me that the long and difficult winter season is over. In the treetops, the birds parade and chirrup in chorus. It's the season of love. All the songs come together in the canopy to form a single great symphony, the sound of happiness. *winter is over*

Further down, the roe deer and I are preparing our territories, nibbling a few seasonal specialities along the way. Courage, Chévi's half-brother, is a very young buck born of the union of Six-Points and Dew, his new partner. Courage, rather gentle by nature, tries to prolong his winter friendships with his companions. His sister, Lila, also by Dew, has an adjacent territory given to her by her mother. That will help her avoid the amorous advances of the neighbouring males. Every day Courage marks his territory a little more, refines his markers and defends them vigorously against the other bucks that are roaming around. Weeks pass and he manages to conquer a little parcel of just over five hectares, not bad for a buck his age.

One morning, in the distance, a noise breaks the fullness of the woodland kingdom. Courage and I decide to go and investigate where those unfamiliar snaps, wails and shrieks are coming from. An invader has entered the wild fortress. This area of forest planted about forty years ago consists of Scots pines, amid which some beautiful old birches, beeches and oaks have survived. In its depths we discover an impressive machine, a kind of tractor mounted on eight enormous, toothed wheels, and with a mechanical arm. At the end of this arm are chainsaws and a huge iron jaw. The machine encircles the tree, grabs it, cuts it from the base, lifts it effortlessly, strips its trunk from base to tip, then severs the head of the tree and cuts it into long pieces to form a pile of logs before moving on to the next tree. The speed of destruction is such, and the noise so intense, that I imagine I can hear the trees crying. Courage, terrified by the presence of this beast on his territory, runs off, barking. For three days the young buck refuses to mark his territory. Three days during which this mechanical monster finishes its work.

Once calm has been restored, we go back to that area to take stock of the changes. The machine has devastated everything. In place of the haven of peace and quiet, burgeoning with food, where squirrels, dormice and birds had built their nests, we discover the silence of a bleak plain. The

*devasted everything
The trees are gone*

engine has razed everything to the ground. Only one rotten tree trunk has been spared in the name of biodiversity. A little label will be fastened to it some months later. Maurice Barrès, in *La Grande Pitié des Eglises de France* (*The Great Pity of the Churches of France*), writes:

> Do you know this kind of anguish, this protest that forms within the depths of our being [...] every time we see a spring sullied, a landscape degraded, a forest cleared or simply a fine tree felled without replacement? What we feel then [...] is something other than merely the loss of a material asset. We feel invincibly that our complete expansion needs vegetation, freedom, life, happy animals, untrapped springs, rivers that do not run down pipes, forests without metal wires, timeless spaces. We love woods, fountains, vast horizons for the services that they give us and for more mysterious reasons. A pinewood burning on the hills of Provence is a church being blown up. A little ravine in the Alps, a bare flank of the Pyrenees, stretches of desert in the Champagne, limestone plateaus, moorlands, the scrubland of the central plateau corresponding in our minds to those village squares where our steeples are crumbling.

I observe Courage, who I have never seen so nervous. He looks from right to left and then from left to right at what was once his territory, he sniffs the air, filled now with a smell of burned oil. He takes a step forward, hesitates for a long time and then gives in. Despondent, he is filled with terrible anxiety. I see by his desperate expression that with his territory destroyed, his shelters no longer exist, food will now be difficult to find and he will no longer be able to participate in the mating season.

Courage finds himself without protection in the territory of his competitors. No doe is going to want a male without a territory, unable to give her a peaceful place of refuge. Unable to recreate a new domain in such a short time, then chased from territory to territory by the other bucks, Courage spends the summer in a thicket measuring five square metres. The absence of food of any quantity or variety is destroying him physically and psychologically. His miserable life, the terrible conditions in which he lives, lead him to abandon caution at the risk of his life. He is exhausted and thin, he loses his fur, parasites invade his body and I'm worried that he will become ill. He cries, groans and waits for the autumn, a season when winter friendships are reborn. I've never seen a roe deer in such a poor state of health.

The foresters' lack of consideration for the forest and its inhabitants concerns me deeply. A forest is above all a community of trees that welcomes other vegetable and animal communities. When the woodland balance is disturbed, all those communities are weakened. The forest reflects life as a whole: complex, mysterious, changing. It gives its inhabitants resources, protection, shade, comfort, beauty and, most importantly, it is of great biological importance. I am able to live with the roe deer and the other wild animals not because I'm applying scientific knowledge, but because I've penetrated

forestry leads to inbalance affecting all of nature

their secrets, understanding one of the most magnificent works of nature: the forest. We don't learn a language by translating word for word. We learn it by virtue of the subtlety of its idiom, the way of life of the inhabitants of the country who speak it, without comparing it with what we know of our own language. I have the good fortune to live with wild animals, because I don't translate nature, I speak it.

The present method of forestry management is not adapted to nature, because the damage caused by clear-cut logging is turning into a real catastrophe for roe deer, which are very attached to their territory. Game and forestry management needs to adapt to natural laws. Man has created artificial conditions of forest life for my companions by planting forests the way you might plant peas. The very valleys, the clearings, the terrains that man sees as being 'of poor quality' give my forest friends the irregularities that they seek in the landscape. Today the logging industry, with its mechanical felling practices, its industrial rhythm and its reforestation methods in monotonous tracts of forest covering hundreds of thousands of hectares, leads to an imbalance among cervids, forcing them to wander among cultivated fields, orchards and young plantations.

We are witnessing a massive exodus of populations fleeing forest environments. With the mechanisation of logging in the 1990s, the plains of Beauce and Eure-et-Loir were home to very few roe deer. Today, they live in copses in groups of between five and ten individuals throughout the day, waiting for dusk and dawn to go and forage in the fields. In the vines,

the roe deer have had to
into orchards & gardens due to
quantity & quality of food due to killing the trees

in Charente-Maritime, no roe deer used to come to feed in cultivated areas. They were a rarity in orchards or gardens. Today the forest no longer offers them the variety, the quality or the quantity of the food that they need, and offers even less protection. Roe deer are more at home in undergrowth and at the edge of the forest than they are in the depths of the woods, but man, with his constant need for urbanisation, is colonising the valleys and eating into their environment. If forests grow naturally, let us look at the artificial clearings that we are making deep within them. There is no point putting huge pressure on the deer population in order to control them, because they are already under attack from the natural predation of foxes and buzzards, which eat young fawns; in some regions, it is lynxes and wolves which take over, not to mention sickness and, more often than we imagine, stray dogs.

However, a numerically fair distribution is being established between deaths and births, so that the number of roe deer remains more or less constant in a given place. One of the ways to correct our poor management would be to keep the most territorial adults while limiting the density of roe deer to the capacity that the environment can accommodate. Then the principle of self-regulation of the species will settle gently, generation after generation, because animals are not suicidal and they don't eat more food than nature can offer. Animals should be allowed to eat in peace throughout the day with thickets arranged regularly across the forest to avoid areas with too high a concentration of wild animals. Forests of deciduous trees with few conifers should be planted to encourage

Animals should be allowed
to eat in peace through out the
day

vegetation on the ground. Organising clearings near bramble patches, for example, with undergrowth in which berry-growing bushes should be planted so that they can find sloes, haws, blueberries and other fruits. Those clearings, or those forest edges, should be welcoming, and the grasses so beloved of roe deer should be allowed to grow to full maturity, and timber varieties should be maintained to produce forest fruits.

Every stage of a forest's evolution has its animals. Hares, partridges, voles, buzzards, martins, weasels, foxes and badgers. The more the forest grows and the denser it gets, the more we plunge into its heart, the more we will see large animals like boar. We should see the trees of the forests as a bond with the other animals that live on the planet. Foresters should return to more humane methods of logging, respect natural cycles and give something more interesting and more tasty to the other animals that also live off this habitat, so that they are less interested in the trees that we want to use. Nature is not a financial deposit, it's an asset shared by all animals, man included.

Foresters need to be more humane in their methods of logging.

Nature is a shared asset by all animals including

Trees — should be replaced + not taken down in such larg quantities.. fruit bushes should be planted —

18

One night, when everything is calm, I decide to go home. What I want most of all is a hot shower. I don't know why, but I've had a kind of premonition. There are no stars tonight. A light wind blows in the tops of the Scots pines, which give off a fresh scent of resin. I walk along a little path that leads down towards the forestry building in the valley, on the edge of the forest. I cross a slope where foxes and badgers have dug their earths. I come across Valloux, an old roe deer friend, with his partner Noelle, who are playing at jumping into huge shell holes from the Second World War. They both live along a power line that has recently been built. A huge clearing about a hundred metres wide and several kilometres long now passes through their territory. The ponds have dried up and several hundred hectares of beech trees have disappeared. Just think, this was once all forest . . .

I continue on my way until I reach the undergrowth. I

find myself on a small, asphalt forest road. I walk over the cattle grids recently installed to stop the animals leaving the forest, something that has become part of an enclosure system set up the full length of the forest. The red deer won't be browsing in the meadows in the autumn any more. It's a while since I left the forest. I'm used to the sounds, the smells and sensations of this environment, to which I have adapted completely. As I reach the edge of the forest, the wind changes, the smells are no longer the same, the air is less humid. I catch a scent of grass. The wind is stronger than in the forest, and passes through all my layers of jumpers, making me shiver. I continue on my way across the plain while the forest calls to me. It's like leaving a girlfriend on the station platform and feeling, as the train pulls away, that you will never see her again. I walk on the pavement, along the dimly lit street. The front gate to the house is double-locked, so I climb over it. At the front door I put my key in the lock and it sticks. I can't open it. I decide to try the little garage door and then pass through a second door that lets me into the house. I go to the fridge: it's empty. I look in the different food cupboards, they're empty, too. Some are even locked. I would later learn that the food had been hidden. I leave with tears in my eyes. I know it's the last time I'll be coming to this house. I walk at a jog, without turning around, to get back as quickly as possible to the ones that I now think of as my real family: the roe deer.

As soon as I reach the forest I look for Chévi, my precious friend, but can't find him. I spend the whole morning looking

The house is locked
+ the food has been hidden
last time he goes home   *Deer Man* 139

for him, without success. The hours pass, and a wave of
depression hits me. I absolutely need to tell him of my pain.
I walk back and forth along his usual routes, without seeing
him. I take a little break in the clearing – I haven't eaten anything, and nothing would have stayed down anyway. In the
early afternoon, physically and emotionally exhausted, I set off
for another part of the forest where he and I are in the habit
of relaxing. It's then that I spot his silhouette. He is there,
upright, proud. He studies me. I run to him, full pelt, and hug
him. With both hands around his neck I start weeping on his
shoulder. He stands motionless for several minutes. I feel his
heart beating against my cheek, and he rests his muzzle on
my shoulder. The warmth of his body does me good. His fur
bristles as if he is shivering, then he starts licking my face. I'm
so happy to see him, to be his friend. I'm convinced that he
senses my unhappiness.

Roe deer have this ability to feel emotions, to tell the difference between good and evil, or between those who wish
them well and those who wish to do them harm. Disgusted
by my own species, which savagely kills my friends, destroys
their environment and lacks respect for the forest, and
wounded by the attitude of those around me, from that
moment I determine to spend as long as possible in complete
autonomy, living off the forest without returning to the
inhuman human world, which I definitely don't understand.
Chévi is the most intelligent roe deer that I know, he doesn't
judge me, he's sensitive to my distress, he always comes to my
aid when I need him. There's something 'human' about his

Hug him & weep. He sense
my unhappiness + licks my face

behaviour, in the noble sense of the term. He's more than a friend, he's a brother, and without succumbing to anthropomorphism, I've discovered a non-human person that I hold in incredible esteem.

He disgusted with
his species that
kill his friends
Destroy their habitat
lack respect for life
+ nature

He discovered in Chevi
a non-human person that
he held in incredible
esteem

19

Time passes and Chévi develops a magnificent set of antlers. They grow quickly, and my friend starts finding their tips itchy. Sometimes when he comes to me to be stroked he takes advantage of the moment to rub them against my arm, my leg or my rucksack. Other times it's against Fern. When he does that he rubs his head against her fur and then, clumsily, against her face. Fern recoils a little, she doesn't like it, but in the end she lets him do it because she realises that it eases the itching.

The way a deer's antlers grow is nothing like that of a cow's horns, which have a living bony core, which explains why they grow all the time. In roe deer, the bone is covered by a kind of skin called velvet. That velvet is run through with many blood vessels that bring the nutrition necessary for the growth of the bone. As they begin to grow, the antlers are extremely sensitive, then that sensitivity fades a little with time, but only disappears completely when they have finished growing.

During the first six months in the life of a young male fawn, the bony pedicles form, to be replaced in February by little horns which will be followed by the first antlers the following year. They finish growing before April. What is incredible is that the growth of the antlers is regulated by a hormone, the production of which depends entirely on sunlight. The velvet appears in winter, while the male hormones are non-existent. In the spring, the hormone, when secreted again, halts the growth. The antlers solidify and the velvet atrophies. The roe deer has only to get rid of it by rubbing his head.

Beneath the velvet the antlers are white, but the tree sap on which the deer rubs them gives them a honeyed or brownish colour. A roe deer that rubs its antlers against a beech tree will give them a light colour, while a deer that rubs them against a conifer will turn them almost black. At first the antlers will be covered with little protuberant bumps which have the same effect on the trees as a cheese grater. Within a short time those pearlings (as they are known) are smoothed out. Needless to say, foresters take a dim view of roe deer at that point, because in trying to shed the velvet they damage trees intended for logging. But the percentage of trees affected remains extremely low, and if they are not cut within the year they will be used the year after. By May, all antlers should have been stripped of velvet, and the oldest bucks will have got rid of it by March. The velvet that falls to the ground soon turns white, and rodents eat it for the calcium.

When Chévi encounters another buck he presents his antlers, shakes his head and sometimes engages in head-to-head

Chévi. I never photograph an animal with which I haven't bonded in some way, because I want their eyes to express the friendship we have for one another.

Photograph only those he has bonded with.

combat. The antlers can't really be seen as a weapon, since they are rarely used for self-defence; flight is more prudent. While a deer can run at a hundred kilometres an hour, its predators seldom get above twenty. More than anything, the antlers represent a beautiful ornament that it is considered stylish to wear in the spring to subdue your rivals in the eyes of a pretty little doe.

The growth of the antlers stops with the loss of the velvet. Then, in the autumn, the natural weakening of the cells of the coronet (the junction where the antlers meet the skull) leads to their loss. They fall all by themselves when the deer runs or rubs itself against a tree. It's worth noting that the age of the individual has no influence on the size of the antlers. A deer like Six-Points has a very large territory, and it's easy for him to find a rich and varied source of food. That's why he has such grand antlers.

We continue our territory-marking path and set off in search of different rubbing spots. We come across Chocotte, who doesn't have very impressive headgear. His antlers look stunted. They are still covered with velvet, but something has gone wrong in the course of their growth. Antlers grow very quickly, and when they aren't yet solidified they can undergo all kinds of traumas and accidents. This is the case with Chocotte this year. His left antler, damaged by a bramble bush when it was still growing, is now covered with unsightly skin that complicates his life. Luckily, this malformation will be shed in the autumn like any other antler, and the next set will not bear the scar of the incident. However, in some more serious cases resulting from an illness, a bullet wound, an abrasion or something else, it can really be disastrous, because the cycle of antler growth is controlled by a very fragile hormonal balance. An ill-timed wound can have serious consequences for their growth, and therefore affect the marking cycle and finally compromise the deer's social life.

The antlers fall all by themselves in the autumn + grow again.

20

In midsummer, I bump into Fern, spread out on the ground in a path of ferns. The heat is intense, and she is relaxing in the sunlight. I can't help comparing her to the little starlets tanning themselves on the beaches of the Mediterranean. At last she gets up and makes straight for Chévi's territory. I always follow her as best I can, because she moves quite quickly. She slips among some brambles, sniffs the different layers of air to work out where Chévi has got to, and then continues her quest. She finds him, and her attitude changes completely. Her gait is both slower and more determined. She stops in front of Chévi, who still looks at her quite affectionately. He approaches, and the damsel pretends to ignore him. He tries a little embrace, without success, turns around her, and then his muzzle slides under the tuft on Fern's rear, making her shiver. She gives a little jump, shakes her head, looks at him and gallops a few metres. Chévi follows her, and she stops abruptly. He comes up behind her at full speed, arches his back to avoid colliding with her and starts putting his front feet on Fern's back. She sets off again at a gallop, and the game seems to arouse the two turtle doves.

Fern is on heat, and attracts Chévi with the secretion of her scent glands, along with a language made up of peculiar cries. These preliminaries consist of checking the physical strength of the buck, and thus naturally selecting the strongest genes to make good, sturdy little fawns. Roe deer are quite polygamous, but Chévi and Fern, like Six-Points with Star, depart from the rule, not by becoming monogamous but by favouring each other in their territory. So Fern rejects the advances of other males and generally avoids gallivanting around in other territories.

Chévi and Fern's amorous little game consists of long and passionate pursuits that end up in a circular run around a tree, a log or a rock. The game lasts until the two lovebirds finally form a little path of beaten earth around the tree, called the witch's ring, on which my poor friend the buck whinnies, groans and even barks to warn competitors who, equally aroused by this little dance, might imagine that they can join in. It's not even worth thinking about.

Make no mistake: at this stage it's the doe who calls the tune and decides where coupling will take place. If the poor, amorous buck gives up or collapses with exhaustion, she will find another one and bring him back to the same mating spot. This isn't the case with Chévi, who doubles his efforts to make sure such a thing doesn't happen. A moment later, Fern is ready to receive Chévi. She stops running around the tree, and Chévi takes advantage of that to mount her several times, obviously a certain pleasure, until the frolicking comes to an end. With a bit of luck, Fern will lead him in the same game tomorrow, the day after and all the days that follow, and that can go on until the end of August, bearing in mind that the oestrus period only lasts two or three days.

In Europe, the fertilisation of does takes place from the middle of July until the end of August, during the rutting season. As soon as it is fertilised, the egg begins to divide and goes on 'floating' in the womb for about six weeks before developing very slowly until December. This little collection of cells is then implanted in the uterine wall, and the development of the foetus begins. This process, called deferred implantation does not exist in any other cervids, and only in a few mammals, including badgers, martens, weasels and stoats. The foetus grows rapidly until the birth of the fawns, nine to ten months after fertilisation. During the forty weeks of gestation of a little fawn, the growth of the embryos needs only twenty, and since nature is perfect, a doe that goes unfertilised in the summer can be fertilised in a secondary rut that takes place between November and December. In that case, the implantation is not deferred and the birth occurs quite normally in the late spring. When the time comes, Fern will probably give birth to one or two fawns that will stay with her until the following spring.

A few days later I come across Magnolia, who is playing the same game. She is 100 per cent polygamous, and so are

Magnolia. A real seductress with a flashing eye. More doe than mother, she finally gives birth to Haw, who will meet a tragic fate.

her partners like Bobois, Chocotte, Harry and many others. Magnolia has led the dance for several seasons without ever producing offspring. She attracts the bucks, seduces them and brings her suitors to the mating spot at a rapid pace until . . . they're exhausted. The poor things always give up in the end. And if by chance she happens upon a more persistent deer than the average, at the moment of mating she disappears. This time I expect the same drama to play out, too. That said, there's something that intrigues me. The territories have been established, Magnolia is on heat and three fine bucks are lying a few metres away from each other, which is far from usual. Magnolia brings along her first suitor, Harry. A few hours pass. Harry is about to give up. That's when I see Bobois trotting towards Magnolia. Harry leaves the witch's circle and Bobois hurries towards Magnolia. Harry goes off and lies down next to Chocotte without any conflict. Magnolia plainly hasn't noticed the funny business and goes on circling the little tree trunk. A short while later – off we go again – Bobois leaves the circle and Chocotte replaces him. I smile at this scene from a Feydeau farce. I can see that Magnolia is starting to get tired, and that she no longer knows how to escape this situation. She doesn't have the strength to run off to abandon her suitor. Then she gives up, stops, puts herself in the coupling position, head lowered, belly contracted and body rigid. Chocotte starts his frolicking and mounts her several times, then Bobois gets into position, mounts her as well, and then it's Harry's turn. All three of them start several times and seem satisfied with their pact.

Magnolia didn't choose this little game, or to have fawns next year. After all these years I'm still surprised by the adaptability of roe deer, capable of abandoning the most elementary natural laws to achieve their ends.

21

Since the end of the summer, Terylle, the little vixen, has been defining her territory, which is enormous, occupying seven square kilometres. She and her partner, whom I have called Vulpes, defend it against intruders. It's the third year that she's been with the same partner. Sometimes I see them hunting together, but most of the time she's on her own, preferring to hunt alone. Once her territory has been defined and protected, she turns an old rabbit warren into her little home, but Vulpes isn't allowed in. Winter is the mating season for foxes. In the relative nocturnal calm of the forest, I can hear my two lovers shrieking, singing, wailing in the distance. A few hours later I bump into Terylle, who looks chipper; the concert given by Vulpes has plainly charmed her. For a few days they don't part, they play together, they exhaust themselves in playing breathless games of chase, without taking into account either their surroundings or any potential dangers. Lovers, in short.

My lovely vixen. Terylle was the companion of Vulpes, a fine black fox with whom she had cubs. I lived with her for a while, but I think that life with foxes is less amusing than life with roe deer. Foxes aren't very interested in other animals, and don't try to create interaction.

April comes. I know that my little vixen has given birth in her den. Before, she pulled out some white hairs on her belly in order to reveal her breasts and allow her little ones access to her teats. After a fifty-two-day gestation period, the cubs are born. I can't see them, but I can hear them. As the cubs need maternal warmth, Terylle has to stay with them for two weeks.

During that time she depends entirely on Vulpes, who brings her an impressive amount of food. The fox seems less good at housekeeping, because a pile of organic detritus accumulates at the entrance to the den. Once the four weeks have passed, only two cubs have survived natural selection. It's their first outing from the mouth of the den. Now that the milk reserves are exhausted, solid food (fieldmice, shrews, beetles, etc.) will be their only source of nourishment. Terylle, now very thin, goes off hunting while the two little ones play. They are boisterous, playful and very curious. When she comes back, she brings food, sometimes buries some for later and then deals with her two offspring. She licks them constantly, because the cleaner their fur the better insulated they are from the cold. Sometimes I lie and watch them with Chévi, who is also curious about all the comings and goings. They are fearless, and come and play at our feet. Their eyes are deep blue, and their faces turn red at the same time as their little muzzles lengthen.

Six months have passed and I now regularly come across the cubs walking alone in the forest. They are weaned and already look like adults. The little male has been chased from the territory by his parents; his sister left of her own accord shortly before. Magnolia, the skittish doe, has had a fawn that I've called Cénèle (Haw). She is a little female, overflowing with spirit and curiosity. I can't tell who the father is, she had so many suitors. Magnolia lives quite far from Terylle and doesn't have anything to fear from Vulpes either. So I watch Haw growing up like lots of fawns before her.

One morning, when she is less than three months old, I

hear her crying in the distance. Her voice is plaintive. She is running frantically in all directions. I approach her and see a magnificent fox in hunting posture. He's a male. I recognise him: it's one of Terylle's cubs. He has clearly established his territory not far from his parents, and he's attacking one of my friends. I look around for Magnolia, who is supposed to defend her child, but she's not there. I get closer, saying to myself that my presence will drive the predator away, but I'm quite wrong. The young fox knows me very well, and remains concentrated on his first thought: having Haw for dinner.

For the first time I'm confronted with the dilemma of life and death. Do I save Haw from the jaws of a predator, or accept the law of nature in all its cruelty? After all these years, is my place still that of a mere spectator, or have I become an agent within the woodland kingdom? As I come forward, I realise that Cénèle is seriously wounded in the throat and the back legs. She calls her mother, who doesn't come. What on earth is going on? Magnolia should be running to help her. The young fox jumps on Haw, bites her belly and sinks his teeth into her neck to bring her down. My young friend won't be getting up again. I can still chase away the predator that has seriously wounded its prey. But to what end? To see Cénèle die from her wounds in front of me? I can't do anything, I arrived too late. And I have to accept it. Overwhelmed, I choose to leave, to avoid witnessing something that's unbearable to me.

I don't understand why Magnolia isn't there. Does are devoted mothers, and I'm surprised by this behaviour. When I find her at last, she's groaning and making little whispering sounds to call her daughter. She obviously lost her trail. She's a very young doe, inexperienced and very clumsy. She's also been suffering for some time from a sort of allergic rhinitis, which must affect her sense of smell. She sniffles all the time, and her nose seems to be blocked. Cénèle was her only daughter, and I notice the distress in the eyes of my poor friend. Making little cries and groans, I invite her to follow me to the scene of the disaster. Once we get there, I observe her grief. She understands that her daughter is dead. She looks around, finds the fox and runs after him, but it's already too late. It will take Magnolia several weeks to get over her ordeal.

22

Fern is walking in a grove, nibbling at the ferns and a few scattered reeds, then she makes her way towards the clearing that offers her ample quantities of small plants. A few metres away, her attention is particularly attracted by a replantation. The logged section has allowed the first colonising trees to regenerate, like birch, hazel, ash, whitethorn and other ligneous or semi-ligneous species. My friend takes advantage of natural coppicing, which provides an incredible variety of young twigs, some of them replete with tender leaves and succulent buds. But Fern doesn't just want to eat, she's also looking for a place where she can hide her little fawns, because I can tell from her rounded flanks that she is expecting little ones. In some very precise spots she leaves marks to define her home range, which she will defend as best she can. It's here that she will give birth and bring up her young. Chévi and Fern have quite a sizeable range, about forty hectares in total, in which all their activities are played out. The other bucks and does are tolerated there. This range guarantees them a supply of food, shelters, some calm and well-located places where they can rest in peace, all criss-crossed by a formidable network of paths. Chévi, for his part, marks his territory rigorously and defends it jealously. It's a kind of district within their home range, which of course overlaps with Fern's zone of activity.

In early May, Fern gives birth in the middle of a meadow. She has only one daughter, who I call Pollen. I leave them in peace for the first few weeks; in any case I'm kept busy during the day by marking territory with Chévi. One afternoon, my best friend joins Fern and her daughter. I walk behind them without a care in the world. Fern is leading, followed by Chévi and then by her daughter. We pass along a logging track where there's a plantation of Scots pines and the air feels milder. Conifers actually have the advantage of conserving heat. The sun warms us, and we look for a suitable place to rest. All of a sudden I'm paralysed by an unpleasant hissing sound. The noise comes from the ground – a snake. I nearly stepped on it, and it doesn't seem too pleased. It's in defensive position, its head slightly raised, and it's not moving. I stand completely motionless, as the roe deer have taught me, my leg raised, frozen in the moment. The snake isn't calming down and I see my friends moving away. I try to groan like a fawn to call to them and tell them of my distress, but neither Pollen nor Chévi pays attention and Fern seems a bit too far away to hear me. Luckily she turns around for a moment. Pollen has stopped as well. They both look at me. I go on groaning with my best imitation of the cry of a frightened fawn. Fern retraces her steps, passes by Chévi and comes towards me. Seeing the snake, she lowers her head. She keeps on coming slowly forward, cautiously, raising her hooves very high. Now she is level with the reptile, which probably hasn't noticed her arrival. She walks behind it, raises her front hoof and violently strikes the snake, which starts to try to get away. Fern pursues it and goes on striking it, aiming at its head. The poor creature is hurled around in all directions like a scrap of rubber tyre. It must be dead by now, but Fern goes on stamping and stamping until she's sure she's finished it off. Then she comes back to see Pollen, gives her a few affectionate licks and resumes her place at the head of the procession. I was in luck. Chévi, his curiosity aroused, comes and looks at the lifeless snake, sniffs it and goes back towards Fern from time to time, and looks at me for approval. I don't think he's ever seen his partner act so violently, but Fern, like all other does, hates snakes, even more because the little ones are around. I'm glad she took this initiative, even if the snake was more frightened than me, and would have left of its own accord after a moment. I'm alive and relieved; thanks, Fern.

Chévi and Fern go on living their lives with their daughter. One fine morning, towards the end of spring, something unexpected happens. Something unexpected that goes by the name of Magalie. This magnificent and experienced doe is Sus's sister. I don't know why, but she has left her area of activity above the forest to come into our sector. I notice that Magalie has huge flanks, and she, too, is pregnant. Since

Fern has already given birth, and her territory is already marked, I imagine that Magalie will go back to her own territory to give birth. Sadly, not a bit of it. Magalie is very territorial, and even if her face makes my heart thump, I have to admit that she has a terrible personality. While I'm spending the morning with Fern and Pollen along a forest track, Magalie approaches. Fern doesn't say anything. She comes forward a little more, sniffs me and then makes her way towards Fern. Chévi's girlfriend, who is every sociable, tries to give Magalie a few licks. Suddenly Magalie starts barking and running resolutely at Fern. Fern stops, stands her ground and tries to see her off, but Magalie, who is the stronger, manages to make her run off. After this long battle, I'm left alone with Pollen and we wait for Fern to return, but it's Magalie who comes back. Pollen, frightened, is breathing in fits and starts and hides her head between her front legs. She's petrified. Magalie doesn't seem aggressive, and pays no attention to Pollen. We wait for a long time and then hear Fern calling us, or, rather, calling her daughter. Running in a straight line, Pollen plunges into a nearby patch of forest to join her mother while Magalie watches us moving away. Fern, expelled from her territory, will not return. Magalie gives birth in high grass, also to a single fawn, a little female that I call Clara.

Months pass. Clara and Pollen become friends. Magalie is more curious about me than she was before, a rare thing among does. In general it's easier for me to unblock psychological obstacles in males, because they have a higher level

Magalie. She considered me a trusted friend. She even made me the unofficial nurse to Sloe and Hope.

it takes 2X as long to bond with the female. They more fearful & take more to trust.

of testosterone. That hormone gives them a bit more self-confidence and makes them feel stronger. With females it takes me twice as long, because they notice things more, they tend to be protective, guided by their maternal instinct, even when they have no young. They're more psychological, and more inclined to be fearful. Magalie isn't at all like her brother Sus. She approaches, observes and understands quickly, and I easily establish a kind of empathy with her.

Magalie spends the autumn with Fern, Chévi, me and other deer who join us: Pond, Bobois, Magnolia, Courage and Sus. We form a fine little group of eleven individuals with Pollen and Clara, and take advantage of our winter friendships to have adventures and explore new parts of the forest. Even though roe deer are home-loving creatures, we cover about five kilometres a day in search of new territory. We play along the various fringes of the forest, running, jumping and hurtling along the big hills just behind the forest ranger's house. We negotiate the barbed wire fence of a meadow full of lush grass and enjoy a few moments of pure happiness.

While my friends chew the cud, I rest among them. Courage gets up to nibble some leaves. All of a sudden, right in the middle of the meadow, he takes a few jumps and stops. He starts again, leaping more than a metre into the air. What's got into him? Nothing. He's playing. He's dancing, he thinks he's a big buck, he has a standoff with a twig sticking out of the field and performs the most incredible pirouettes. He is filled with a happy madness, the joy of life. He calms down a little under the amused gaze of his fellow deer before starting

play is jumping about,

all over again. He throws himself into the air and wiggles his hindquarters at the same time, he kicks his heels at the sky, falls back to the ground and arches his back. The game goes on; he spins around, points his antlers at some imaginary deer and runs around like mad before resuming his capers. After a brief moment of rest, he leaps into the air again, turns around and then lands on the ground with his legs splayed. He's intrigued by everything and amused by trifles, and goes on playing like that for several minutes before finally coming back to lie down near Magalie as if nothing had happened.

We return to the interior of the forest; Pond has a cheeky expression on her face, and even though she's used to seeing me she regularly puts me to the test. In the late afternoon, when she's lying down and everything is calm, she suddenly sets off at a run, stops and observes the reaction of the others, but particularly mine. She is trying to exert a kind of authority over the group, but it doesn't work because roe deer don't have leaders. Besides, since she's a little crazy, no one trusts her. Sometimes she breaks the serene atmosphere of the group. She becomes over-excited, and spends her time teasing the others. I confess that she sometimes gets on my nerves. At the same time she's cute, and her sturdy character promises great things for the future.

The winter passes, spring is on the way, but it's still cold. The few years that I have spent in the forest are starting to do me harm. Because of my drastically reduced diet, I become physically exhausted more quickly than before. It's drizzling, and an icy wind penetrates all the layers of my clothing. Since

Roe Deer do not have leaders

I'm in good company, and trusted by my roe deer friends, I decide to doze for a few minutes. I take shelter from the wind behind a big tree. The rain comes pelting down, but I ignore it. In fact, a band of low pressure is on the way and the temperature is about to plummet. I start dozing off and sink quickly into a deep sleep. My body temperature drops. *exhausted*

When I wake up I don't know where or who I am. To make matters worse, all my limbs are paralysed. I can't get up. Chévi comes to see me and starts licking my face as he usually does after his nap. His little hot tongue running over my face wakes me a little and drags me from my torpor. It's then that I become aware of where I am. I see the big shining eyes of my friend, with his little nose pressed against mine. I try to get up, but I'm fixed to the ground. My legs are heavy, and I feel as if my commands are going unanswered. With one final effort, I grab hold of a branch and try to stand up. My heart pounds in my chest, my head is heavy, the landscape is spinning around me and my whole body is numb. I throw up. I try to take a few steps to warm up and take a candle out of my pocket, which I manage to light after striking several matches. I put it on a handful of dead leaves that struggle to catch. I add some little twigs that I always carry in my rucksack for emergencies. The flames start rising and I begin to lose my chill. I put on a little log which I cut with my knife so that the fire doesn't go out. There we go, I'm getting my spirit back. Chévi and the others approach the fire, which I go on feeding, and then we spend the evening together. I'm cross with myself for letting myself go like that. It could have cost me my life. When you live outside in difficult conditions, you can't avoid all dangers, but good organisation and good preparation can really save your life. That little scare was like an electric shock. It wasn't the first time that had happened to me, but it had never lasted as long. I want to spend my life with my friends the roe deer, intensively, I don't mind if my life is short. But if I want to save them from the destruction of this world which is losing its mind, I have to stay alive, to tell their story and make the wider public aware of the reality of life in the wild.

living in the forest for years has affected my health.

He feels he wants to spend his life with his friends, even if it is a short one.

23

In order to understand roe deer you have to understand their history, which is sometimes tragically bound up with our own. In prehistoric times, hunting was a pillar of the survival and continued existence of humankind. At first it was played out in big areas of grassland, but the climate change of the time and the rapid growth of trees altered the nature of prey. Red deer, boar, wolves and roe deer took advantage of these huge changes. The growth of animal populations speeded up and men hunted, not only to provide themselves with food, clothes and tools, but also to defend their nascent agriculture. This new activity, of course, influenced the behaviour of animals, and gradually transformed the forest into a refuge for these hounded animals. Still, archaeological research finds very little evidence of the presence of roe deer on human menus. Perhaps roe deer didn't damage crops enough for them to take an interest. Perhaps the intelligence of these animals, their solitary lifestyles and their ability to escape danger made them in a way inaccessible. We don't know.

Until the high Middle Ages, kings organised hunts that were supposed to protect harvests from damage caused by wild animals, with peasants acting as beaters. The hunting of red deer was common practice, while for some historians the hunting of roe deer is purely a twentieth-century invention. Then kings and lords turned hunting into a 'leisure activity', and ceased to protect the peasants from the repeated incursions of animals into their fields. A law of 1396 went so far as to ban peasants from hunting, even though the game was damaging their land. Hunting, the main aim of which was to get rid of wild animals, moved away from the interests of the farmers to become a selfish pleasure of slaughter. François I, known as the father of hunters, protected the animals against agricultural interests. As a result a split arose between the king and the people over the simple pleasure of hunting.

If this passion of kings had the advantage of preserving our finest forests, it deeply altered their appearance. Paths were traced within them to make it easier to get around in the mountains. Star-shaped roads were created, going off in several directions from a central point. In 1763, a very precise map called 'The King's Hunts' was published, to identify the countless trails that ran through the forest ranges and provide orientation. This gave rise to modern cartography, until it became what it is today. Forests became so important that they were granted certain protected privileges. New forests were even planted. In my own part of France, Norman noblemen regulated and sometimes even banned agriculture in certain places so that the forests could grow and their fauna develop.

Forests were no longer useful to human beings as a source of wood or foodstuffs, but only for the leisure of the hunt.

One of the first privileges abolished by the French Revolution of 1789 was the exclusive right to hunt. The social order was broken, and with it the lives of thousands of wild animals, roe deer included. Until then, only kings and nobles were allowed to hunt, and roe deer were left out, if not completely ignored. From the nineteenth century onwards, roe deer were given the status of 'small game' and were not subject to restrictions. Hunting became democratic and in less than a century they disappeared almost entirely from our landscapes. The twentieth century and its two great wars also led to the deaths of many wild animals. It wasn't until 1979, when the so-called 'hunting plan', a series of restrictions on hunting seasons, became obligatory in France, that roe deer were able to breathe a little. The species reproduced and began to stabilise. Except that the post-war reforestation, those monotonous tracts of woodland planted in straight lines, the development of winter crops, the practice of scattering grain for wild animals in forests, and all measures taken at the time to industrialise the country totally destabilised the roe deer biotope. The industrialisation and mechanisation of the rural world are increasingly making wild fauna incompatible with the viability of agriculture and forestry. Roe deer have not changed since the arrival of humans on earth. On the other hand, the cultural modifications of the last few centuries, and particularly the last few decades, have changed the lives of woodland creatures.

industralyation have changed the lives of woodland creatures

Scarcity. Forestry has reduced the amount of available food, and sometimes forces us into cultivated fields or gardens in search of roots and tubers.

Not so long ago, the forest provided just as much food as our fields do now. Neolithic man essentially lived on acorns. In the Middle Ages, acorns were a fruit consumed by the people, used especially in pancakes or bread. They were also used in the distillation of alcohol or as a substitute for coffee. It was the arrival of the potato that marked the end of acorn consumption. Other fruits such as chestnuts, hazelnuts, walnuts, haws, sloes, wild pears, wild cherries and sorb apples were among popular foodstuffs. In the Alps, the stone pine, a conifer that produces large seeds, was used by country people who stored the seeds for the winter, and the undergrowth of those forests was just as rich, if not more so, than many forest trees. Strawberries, raspberries, blackberries and lingonberries were widely consumed. The mushrooms of our forests were famous even in Rome. Ferns were used in former times to stuff mattresses. Beech leaves were used to stuff palliasses poetically known as 'plumes de bois', or 'woodland feathers'. Scattered rushes were used as floor coverings. Since the dawn of time the forest has provided us with resins, lacquers, gums, latex, fruit and wood. Even more than that, this cultural link which binds us to the forest allows us to 'regulate', without really paying attention, the quantity of food available in the same forest. With the help of natural predation, we are also involved in the regulation of animal populations. It's also thanks to this cultural connection that I have been able to keep this adventure going for so long. The problem lies in the fact that we have moved on from gathering nuts and berries to an intensive and destructive system of arboriculture whose

destruction for the sole purpose of PROFIT

sole purpose – at the expense of all the little plants which constituted the greatness and richness of our forests – is profit.

Today, when a roe deer nibbles the terminal bud of a young sapling intended for sale at some point in the more or less distant future, this 'mutilated' sapling, in the eyes of the forester and the logging industry, becomes unviable for commercial exploitation. For this industrial park – still called a 'forest' – to regenerate, investment is made in protective measures such as fences, for example, but these are expensive procedures (€20,000 for about ten hectares). And those fences, often erected in clearings or clear-cut tracts of woodland, lead to a loss of territory and a significant lack of food for the roe deer, which are obliged to move to other areas of forest where they will continue to eat, leading to the erection of still more expensive fences. There are also individual protections for the young plants. They take the form of plastic sleeves or little grilles, and allow fauna to circulate freely, but these protections are often more expensive than the saplings themselves, and do not solve the problem of feeding roe deer.

The forest as it has been colonised by modern man leaves no room for the other species that also live off it. However, it's easy to learn to share, and I'd even say, 'learn to give in order to receive'. If I plant a willow tree of no financial value next to a beech or a spruce, it's the willow that the roe deer will eat, because it's tastier. If I leave bramble patches growing in the 'unexploited' areas of forests, I create a refuge and a protection which will mean that the roe deer don't need to go off to see how they might do better elsewhere. If I leave the grass

The Forest should not be considered an industrial development

in the clearings unmown, the roe deer are less likely to go to the edge of the road to eat it, and so on. The forest should be considered not as an industrial development, but as capital that provides interest of which we can make unlimited use. In our 'fields of trees', roe deer won't stop eating just because we want them to. They interact with the forest. They don't exploit it, they maintain it. They live off it and have no interest in wasting this natural vital resource. There's no point in trying to achieve the ideal density of animals for the wood industry to be preserved from all these wild beasts. There is no need to foster a balance between forest and game; it has never been done and it can't be done, because it is unstable and has varied since the dawn of time. It depends on climate, weather conditions, food supply, predation and many other factors. In our own century, modern industry introduces quotas and overproduces for an advance that is unpredictable. This way of working cannot operate in the context of the forest, or in any natural habitat.

Applying a maximum density of twenty roe deer per hundred hectares has no meaning for animals that live very far away from our commercial rules. It isn't a good enough indicator to establish a balance between nature and industry in a world already greatly troubled by climate change. The annual counts represent only an evolutionary average, not an absolute indicator. No balance can exist when you force a natural environment to become a financial deposit. It's up to the forestry industry to follow natural laws, without which balance is broken. It needs to allow the formation of thickets

Max. density of 20 roe deer per area has no meaning to these precious animals

in the forest and create sanctuaries, practise coppicing, leave natural clearings, encourage natural seeding, reduce the pressure from hunting and allow roe deer to self-regulate. No: man is not useful in this process, he does not replace predators, and needs to know his place.

If animals suffer from this industrialisation of the forest, do walkers and, generally speaking, all the other users of the forest realise the extent of the damage that they are doing to this natural environment? One day it will be too late to react. It's time to accept our responsibilities. There's no point in going to the other ends of the earth to film endangered jungles. Ours are equally biologically importance, and they too are busy dying. A little thought for the forest:

Man,
I am the flame of your hearth in the winter night
And, at the height of summer, the cool shade
    on your roof
I am the bed you sleep on, the frame of your house
The table on which you put your bread, the mast
    for your ship
I am the handle of your hoe, the door of your shack
I am the wood of your cradle and of your coffin
The material of your work and the frame of
    your universe
Hear my prayer: do not destroy me . . .

24

Clara is growing up, and Magalie tries to show her in different ways that it's time for her to go and live her life on her own, elsewhere. But Clara doesn't really seem inclined to get it. Magalie, however, has prepared an adjacent territory for her on which she'll be able to live in safety. There's nothing to be done, the young doe doesn't want to grow up and prefers to stay near her mother. Magalie waits for another few days, but time is pressing, because more fawns are on the way. And then, seeing that her daughter doesn't respond, she finally expels her from her territory as she did with Fern last year. Clara settles in the adjacent territory, where she will go on seeing her mother, who continues to protect her.

A few weeks later, Magalie calves in the same place where she gave birth to Clara. I call the little ones Liberty and Charlie. Magalie introduced me to Clara when she was almost weaned, and it was only then that I started walking behind her. This time, she introduces me to her young only after

Magalie and Sloe. Magalie taught Sloe how to recognise plants. In this part of the forest it was easy to find the plant called yellow archangel, which female roe deer like because it's rich in nutrition. Sloe will need it when she has little ones of her own.

two months. I'm flattered. Her posture suggests that she was proud to let me meet them. I think she's holding me in greater esteem because I'm not trying to see her children at any price, and she likes the way I let her have some rest.

The year passes quietly and then, the following spring,

starts all over again. The young roe deer are politely invited to leave their mother to go and make their lives elsewhere. Since Liberty is the little female, she regains a territory adjacent to Magalie's. Clara has been able to use her territory for two years in a row. Charlie isn't favoured in the same way, because he's a male. He has to set off in search of a territory, or find a roebuck to act as mentor, friend or father. He chooses Courage as his tutor. That make sense, because they spent the winter together, they're bosom buddies, and Courage seems to be in love with Magalie.

When the logging industry puts intense pressure on roe deer territory, the size of their spaces declines and young deer can no longer settle outside the place where they were born. They adapt to the situation by avoiding all confrontation with their neighbours, maintain an overly close relationship with their mother, and end up settling in their mother's territory. This 'philopatric' behaviour creates groups of roe deer which expand via couplings with brothers and sisters from the previous year, or indeed with any close relative. This leads to an increase in affection, lower levels of aggression and a reduction in the size of the home range.

Spring passes quickly, and the summer that follows is equally fine. Courage manages to court Magalie, who is happy to accept the advances of this young suitor. Together, they will have two fawns, a male I call Hope and a terribly cute female I call Sloe. This year, Magalie doesn't wait. As soon as the birth-markings have disappeared, she introduces me to her two lovely fawns, each of which weighs a good kilo and a half as far as I can tell. I take great pleasure in following them on their walks, and one day I understand that Magalie, when she's tired, gives me her little ones to look after. As a general rule, does don't go more than two hundred metres from their offspring. But Magalie is a well-organised mother. Exhausted after the delivery, she has recruited me as an unofficial nurse to her kids, and while madame is off going about her day-to-day business, feeding in the long grass, I'm left with two very unruly little fawns. Since Mum isn't there, they only very rarely obey my barks. They run in all directions, catcalling to one another. Hope tries to knock his sister over by putting all his weight on her. Sometimes she collapses, bringing her brother down with her with an indescribable racket.

Luckily Magalie has to return ten times a day to suckle them. She can't store her reserves, and has to pass on to Sloe and Hope the vital energy and the nutrition that she extracts from nature, hence the importance of preserving the quality, the variety and the quantity of the food sources in the forest. Quite simply, it's about the survival of the fawns. Rainfall is important, particularly at the end of spring. And it's water that defines the quality and availability of food. The more water there is, the more food, the richer the milk will be and the better the health of the young. Sloe and her brother grow quickly and put on weight, about a hundred and fifty grams a day for each of them. So Magalie has to produce quality milk in great quantities every day, to ensure that her two fawns can grow by their three hundred grams. Bearing in mind that Magalie only weighs twenty-five kilos, this is an exceptional

My favourite. Sloe is like a female Chévi: intelligent, curious and mischievous, with a real desire to learn about the world around her.

record. It represents the most important maternal investment known among ungulates. Unfortunately, in spite of this complete devotion, the does that live in an area of woodland exploited by man, where trees are regularly clear-felled, can no longer supply either the quantity or the quality of milk necessary for their young fawns. Food such as yellow archangel or nettles becomes scarce. This leads to a high mortality rate among the young, regardless of sex, in the first three months, and it is sad to observe that the fawns go on to have a similar life. When one of them dies of malnutrition in this manner, it gets weaker and sometimes succumbs to the cold in the early morning, when the temperature is at its lowest. A short time later, the death of the second will often be observed.

When my two protégés are satisfied, Magalie comes to see me, and I have the idea of tasting the milk of a roe deer doe. So I stroke her for a long time and then try to move under my friend like a mechanic under a car to reach the double pair of breasts. I gently stroke one teat, pressing lightly, and then the milk flows gently. It's delicious, if you like infused milk. It's like concentrated milk infused with dried flowers and artichokes. The taste is surprising, but not that bad. What's more, roe deer milk is richer in nutrition than cow's or goat's milk. In any case, it was just curiosity, and I'd rather leave it to my little fawns who need it to get big and strong.

Sloe is incredibly intelligent, like a female Chévi. I think Courage's genes must have something to do with it. I've distinguished several families that I've called the Six-Points, from the family of Six-Points, Chévi, Courage and Pollen; the Bordes, of the family of Sus, Magalie and Ponde; the Cobourgs; the Vaulloines; and so on. Each family is unique. There's a kind of lineage with particular characteristics such as the growth of the antlers, elongated muzzles or otherwise, the more or less orange colour of the fur, and a 'face' with recognisable family features. Interbreeding between families sometimes produces roe deer of surprising beauty and intelligence. I notice that the Six-Points family has a very powerful gene; each time, the result is a character like that of Chévi or his father, and now the character of Sloe. The same is true of the Bordes, who are rather reserved, and whose antlers, in the males, grow in a V shape, while in the Six-Points family they tend to grow straight and close together.

I have a lot of fun with Sloe. She sees me as being a bit like her big human brother. I don't replace her twin brother, but she does hold me in very high esteem. Magalie goes off to rest in the sunlight with her son and I stay with Sloe, who doesn't want to move. We let the little family move away and stay resting at the foot of a tree. The light is beautiful and the sun's rays penetrate the canopy. Sloe is lying about ten centimetres away from me, coiled up as usual, her muzzle under her knee. All of a sudden, with an almighty crash, a shadow takes us by surprise: a buzzard plunging down at us. Its claws literally open up my arm and my leg – I can't believe my eyes. The bird of prey looks surprised and confused, as if it wasn't expecting to see me there. Seeing Sloe sleeping, it was tempted by the idea of hunting a fawn. Bad luck that I'm there, and the bird certainly hadn't seen me. I could be said to have saved Sloe from a tragic end. The predator flies off with a shriek. Sloe, still quivering, runs off to find her mother, who isn't far away. There is blood all over my arm, and there's a deep wound in my calf. Magalie sees us arriving terrified. She immediately runs to Sloe and licks her, whispers to her a little, then Sloe calms down and so do I. I take advantage of the moment to pour water from my water bottle over my wounds to clean them. Magalie comes over to me, sniffs at me and licks me. We return to our cover at the end of an emotional day.

Summer and winter pass uneventfully and, in spite of my exhaustion, I remain optimistic about the approaching winter. In fact, there are still some surprises in store for me. We're approaching the winter solstice. The nights are painfully long. Chévi, Fern and Pollen change their territory. They leave the beechwood to go deep into a pine forest where logging is underway. It will bring them tender leaves and buds next spring. Sloe and her brother are still very young, while Pollen is already a beautiful yearling. I go back and forth between the two territories, which are quite a distance from one another. It is now bitingly cold and the weather is getting worse. However, one evening a certain mildness provides balm to my heart. It's raining slightly, but not as badly as I've known in the past. Courage joins Magalie, Sloe, Hope and me. I snooze a little. Sloe lies down just in front of me. When I open my eyes it's snowing. The snow is falling heavily, and Sloe is covered by a thin coating. There isn't a sound in the vast forest, only the faintest crystal tinkling as the flakes touch the ground. I get up to shake off the flakes that are starting to drench my pullover. Still lying down, Sloe licks herself and sometimes tries to sniff a snowflake that falls in front of her. It doesn't stop snowing all night. In the early morning the cold returns. The cloak of snow is not very thick for now, and it isn't yet too hard to find food. One fine sunny day passes, and I use it to rest on some fir-tree branches, in the bright sunlight. Night falls, and the sky is overcast again. Snowflakes whirl in the air, the cold gets a little stronger again and then, after nightfall, the snow begins to fall in abundance. An icy wind from the east freezes me immediately. The snow turns into ice. At daybreak the forest is like a skating rink. The successive layers of snow and ice make the terrain every difficult to negotiate. Magalie and Sloe nearly fall several times, and so do I. The bramble leaves are completely frozen. The does scrape the ground to get rid of the snow and the leaves, then lie down in the hole that they have just dug and rest for a long time.

When climatic conditions become extremely harsh, the roe deer are able to slow down their metabolism. So Sloe stays in front of me, almost motionless all day, and considerably reduces her activity. This phenomenon is explained by the ability that roe deer have to reduce the absorbent surface of their bellies, allowing them to survive major and prolonged climatic events, without feeling the need to eat or move, and without losing lots of weight. A kind of superpower to which, sadly, I don't have access. I look more like a pink flamingo. I lift one leg to get rid of the numbness, then the other, and so on. And the only thing I can do is to move from one territory to the other to see if everyone is all right. But it leaves me exhausted. So I reduce my activity as well, I make a fire to heat some water and warm myself up. The only thing to do is wait patiently for it to pass. I'm starving, but I mustn't think about it. I admire the extraordinary resilience of the little fawns. They look frail and fragile, but they never complain. They set a fine example.

The crisis passes, the wind and rain return with more

clement temperatures and life goes on. This climatic hazard has made me think again about the end of my adventure, torn this time between this wild world with the roe deer that I love so much, but in which I'm gradually withering away, and the need to return to humans to survive and tell the story of my friends.

The harsh / hazardous winter
has made him think torn
between his love for his
friends + the need to
return to humans to survive
+ tell the story of his
friends

The deer are able to slow
down their metabolism
which allows them the ability
to survive climatic events

25

'm tired. I'm losing my strength, I feel that in the very depths of my being. The cold, the snow and the ice of last winter were particularly exhausting. I struggle to find the food that would give me the strength that once ran through my body. My territory is stretched too thin. No leaves, no grass. Everything has been cut down, the wild cherries, the yellow archangel, the nettles. The clearing has been turned into a field of maize. I have to travel for several kilometres to find anything to eat. To make matters worse, everything has been felled on either side of the main trail. Before, there were birch trees, wild cherries, ashes, hornbeams; it was a visual shield behind which we could go walking, seeing the path without being seen. Today, that shield has disappeared, and you can see two hundred metres into the forest.

I'm thinking more and more about bringing this adventure to an end. Not that I want to abandon my friends, I'd rather die side by side with them in the forest than elsewhere among

In a way I could become their spokesman

humans. I know some places where no one would ever find my body. In particular I think of the suffering that my friends endure every day in the face of the disappearance of their territory, and I think it would be good, for both them and me, to relate the things you can experience when you're a wild animal. Without wishing to be pretentious, in a way I could become their spokesman.

Daguet is old, and we spend this early summer morning sleeping to regain our strength, A few hours pass, the sun rises and Daguet wants to cross a very busy forest path. His territory is divided this year, because the young bucks of former years have become more powerful and Daguet's old bones can no longer compete with them. The anarchic growth of his antlers makes me think of the fingers of arthritic old men. His former grandeur is fading and the new generation now sees him as a plaintive old stuffed shirt. He gets up, grooms himself, nibbles a few nearby leaves and then steps cautiously into the path. He wastes a little time on some brambles along the side of the clearing. A few moments later some morning walkers arrive. Daguet lifts his head, observes them for a moment and then comes back, neck stretched, into the undergrowth where we were before. The walkers pass. We stay there for a long time, and then Daguet lies down to chew the cud.

After this moment's rest he gets up and browses, then sets off again towards the forest path. As he crosses, a cyclist comes down the pebbled path at full speed. Once again, Daguet resigns himself to eating a few flowers that grow inside the forest. Time passes, he steps cautiously forward, but as he's

Beech leaves. This is where Chévi was born, but this part of the forest no longer exists. It was subjected to a first cut that got rid of birches, hornbeams, hazels and blackthorns, then a second that cleared the oaks and the other valuable trees, before being subjected to a third clear-felling that left nothing but a desolate landscape.

finally preparing to cross, three moto-cross riders pass at full speed. This time Daguet jumps into the undergrowth, climbs a little slope and watches the bikes disappear into the distance. One step forward, three steps back, and the merry-go-round begins all over again. Every time we try to cross to the other side of that damned road, a walker, a car, groups of tourists or runners take us by surprise and stop poor Daguet from continuing with the marking of his territory.

The day passes, and human activity slowly becomes more sporadic. We go back to the road, and peace seems to have returned. The sun is about to set, and Daguet calms down, taking advantage of the quiet to nibble a few leaves, when I see someone walking their dog in the distance. Daguet sees them too and comes back again. Right, I've had enough. For the first time since I chose to live in total immersion in the forest, I decide to approach the walker.

Daguet his dear freend
has grown old.

26

'Good evening ...'
'Good evening, *monsieur.*'

The walker is a woman. She wears jeans, a white polar jacket and square, metal-rimmed glasses. I look at her Pyrenean mountain dog. I'm worried that it will catch Daguet's scent on me. If it turns aggressive, I risk losing control of the situation and I'm not sure I would know how to react. I adopt an affable air, or at least do my best to.

'I should warn you, there's a big boar out for a stroll a bit further up. For your own safety and that of your dog, you should really turn back.'

'Oh, thank you. You're right. Do you know the forest well?'

'Yes, I'm a nature photographer.'

We talk about animals and the beauty of the forest world as we walk back towards her car, parked in the car park outside the forest, on the edge of the village. She tells me that a road-building project is underway, that the work will start soon, and that the forest will suffer. She seems attached to nature and I don't know why, but I start to talk to her about my friends the roe deer.

'How exciting. You know, you should really exhibit your photographs to tell people about the life of the roe deer.'

A strange feeling fills me. A feeling that I've never felt before. I'm touched by this woman who loves animals and nature. She seems to have a certain interest in defending my friends. We are at nightfall. I return to Daguet, who has finally managed to cross the path. I can't forget the face of that woman who returns regularly to my thoughts. And the memory of her scent doesn't leave me either.

A few months later, I've resumed contact with civilisation, and I'm organising my first exhibition at Les Damps, a little village near Louviers. A crowd of people turn up to study my photographs, but also to catch a glimpse of the strange person who spent seven years, not far from their own homes, surrounded by wild animals, scaring the walkers. When I talk to these people, all my senses are on alert. I can smell their fear, their horror, dread or suspicion. It's very hard for me, the source of anxieties the like of which I hadn't felt for years.

And then, mid-conversation, a few metres away, in front of one of the most beautiful portraits of Chévi, I recognise the form that moved me so a few months before. She smiles at me and comes over.

'Are you the one I met in the forest?'

'Yes, that's me. How are you?'

I immediately understand that my adventure will never be

lonely again. And that she alone will meet my friends. On 31 December, the feast day of the forest, I introduce her to Magalie, Sloe, Hope and Sus. From now on, at least two of us know the extraordinary world of roe deer.

EPILOGUE

The forest is an integral part of the universe of roe deer and human beings. It feeds and it protects, and if each one of us watches carefully over it, that's how it will remain for a long time to come. The forest protects us against the cold of the frozen winter, it softens the heat of blazing summer, eases the violence of the wind, and prevents the advance of the desert. The forest is fertile, it brings us food and medicine. Without it, our landscapes would be nothing but desolation, and life would be reduced to total silence. It is the forest that purifies the atmosphere and allows us to breathe the oxygen indispensable to all living creatures. Without the forest there is no animal life, so let's respect it, let's respect the animals who live there and not, out of selfishness, forget the debt that we have towards it. To live with roe deer is to live with the forest. Man appeared on earth less than a million years ago. In the course of my adventure, I have taken an interest in our little narrative within the larger context of natural history.

Who has never set eyes on a roe deer at a bend in the road? Most observations are fleeting but, with the growth of our cities, peri-urban zones now allow most of us to come across this marvellous animal quite often. However, to come across something is not necessarily to become acquainted with it. Our human activities, by industrialising forestry, interfere in the life of roe deer even on the social level. Anyone who takes an interest in animal life needs to understand what a forest is. Then, faced with the economic and industrial difficulties of our age, I hope that this new approach to roe deer, based on sharing our lives, will allow us to open the door on to a better integration of man with his environment.